HARLEY-DAVIDSON

THE LEGENDARY MODELS

CHARTWELL
BOOKS

HARLEY-DAVIDSON

THE LEGENDARY MODELS

CONTENTS

TEXT
Pascal Szymezak

EDITORIAL PROJECT
Valeria Manferto De Fabianis

EDITORIAL COORDINATION
Laura Accomazzo - Giorgio Ferrero

GRAPHIC DESIGN
Paola Piacco

INTRODUCTION

In the early 20th century, when new technologies and mechanical dreams flourished, many brands of motorcycles and cars appeared on the scene. In fact, at that time more than 150 motorcycle manufacturers were listed in the U.S., including seven based in Milwaukee, Wisconsin. And it is precisely in that city that William Harley and the Davidson brothers set out to build their own motorcycles. Originally, "Harley-Davidson" was a combination of the two founders' names, two men who embodied this motorcycling dream, William Harley and Arthur Davidson. They were eventually joined by the other Davidson brothers, William and Walter.

For those original two, the idea of building a motorcycle had already taken shape in 1901. However, the incredible Harley-Davidson saga would only truly begin in 1903, after various attempts at installing an engine in a bicycle frame. At the end of 1903, the first Harley-Davidson "factory," in actuality a wooden shed measuring roughly 10 feet (3 m) by 15 feet (4.5 m), was built in the Davidson family garden. "Harley-Davidson Motor Co." was painted on the door. But, by the end of 1904, this cottage started to grow, reaching 10 feet (3 m) by 30 feet (9 m) and producing 8 motorcycles in 1904, 16 in 1905 and 50 in 1906. In 1906 a 28-foot (8 m) by 78-foot (23 m) factory was erected on Chestnut Street in Milwaukee, a street that would eventually be renamed Juneau Avenue.

As is the case in most young industries, motorcycle manufacturers in the early 20th century generally only lasted a short time due to economic woes, technological deficiencies or their inability to build a distribution network. However, Harley and the Davidsons were able to gather enough capital for their development, acquired the necessary technical knowledge and developed an outstanding distribution network. Thus, in 1920 Harley-Davidson became the largest motorcycle manufacturer in the world and, in 1953, the only remaining American motorcycle manufacturer after Indian closed its doors.

Harley-Davidson has manufactured motorcycles for over 100 years. This rich history is at the heart of the motorcycle company's special mystique and the reason it is worshiped by millions of fans.

It isn't easy manufacturing a vehicle, but this company, created by a group of fervent friends, has kept this passionate spirit alive, even when the Harley and Davidson families no longer directly presided over the business. It was during one of those dramatic moments that Willie G. Davidson, grandson of one of the founders, joined forces with 12 other people to reacquire the Harley-Davidson Company. With the help of his daughter Karen and son Bill, he is still building on that rich history.

1 THE HARLEY-DAVIDSON LOGO FROM THE EARLY YEARS.

2-3 THE 2008 CVO FXSTSSE2 SOFTAIL SPRINGER.

4-5 VRSCDX NIGHT ROD SPECIAL.

6 THE TANK OF AN ELECTRA GLIDE FROM 1965.

10-11 AN X8A FROM 1912.

12-13 THE 2006 FLST SOFTAIL HERITAGE.

14-15 A 2006 CVO OF THE FLHTCUSE ULTRA CLASSIC ELECTRA GLIDE.

FIRST SINGLE-CYLINDER ENGINES, AND NEW SINGLE-CYLINDER ENGINES

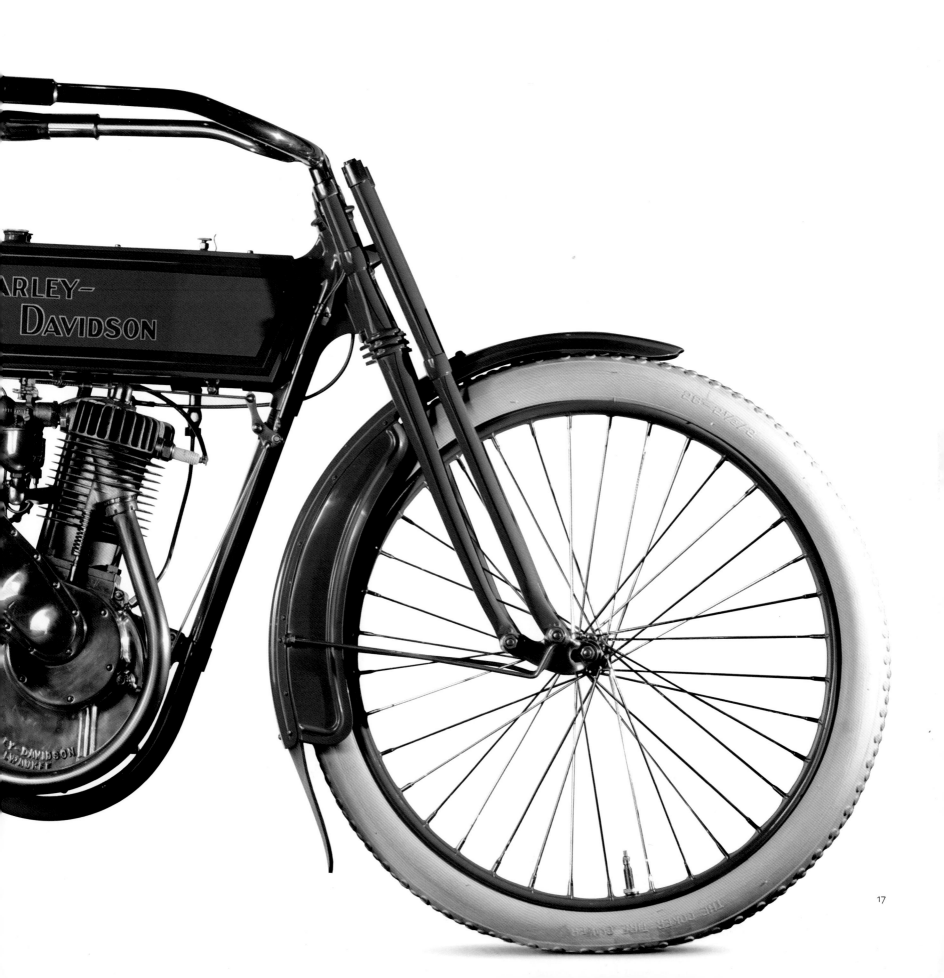

FIRST HARLEY-DAVIDSONS (1903–1905)

According to legend, the real story of Harley-Davidson began in the fall of 1900 with an idea: removing the effort required in riding a bicycle. Evidently others had the same idea, as the ER Thomas Company began producing and commercializing its own version of a two-wheeled power-driven bike in 1901.

As is the case with many motorcycle pioneers, William S. Harley began working, from the age of 15, at a bicycle manufacturing company. In 1901, Harley, then 21, and his friend Arthur Davidson, 20, were employed by the Barth Manufacturing Company, a metallurgical plant based in Milwaukee. Harley worked as a designer and Davidson as a modeler, and the pair shared a common passion: fishing. Their initial idea was to design and build an engine that would have enabled them to quickly and easily reach their favorite places to fish. This engine project, however, soon began to evolve as their interest in a new mode of travel, the motorcycle, grew. The project took up most of their leisure time during the next two years and, helped by friends and members of their families, they would soon produce their initial Harley-Davidson motorcycle, with the first single-cylinder engine, in 1903.

Among the friends who contributed to the first Harley-Davidson single-cylinder engine is Emil Kröger, a German designer who worked in the same factory as the two friends. Kröger had some experience in Europe in this field, having worked on the original prototypes of a De Dion internal combustion engine. By studying the technical magazines of the time, and with the aid of Kröger's experience, Harley and Davidson made an engine in late 1900-early 1901 with a carburetor cobbled together from a tin can and a candle as big as a doorknob. Harley sketched the plans and projects and Davidson made the molds into which the molten metal was poured. Together they manufactured the crankcases, cylinder, crankshaft and pistons (plus the rings, rods and valves with guides). The prototype was a 10.2 cubic inch (170 cc), single four-stroke engine with a 2.125 x 2.875 inch (5.4 x 7.3 cm) bore and stroke, side exhaust valves and "automatic" inlet valves – the engine suction pulled the valve open. The valve inlet opened when the piston descended, creating a vacuum in the cylinder, and closed when it rose. The engine worked, but it sorely lacked power and also leaked oil.

A second model was created, but it was only on the third try that the pair developed a block engine that was sufficiently reliable and efficient to propel a boat. Harley and Davidson installed this engine on a standard bicycle frame and worked on the fuel problem. Another friend, Ole Evinrude, who would later become well-known in the maritime industry, also contributed to the evolution of this engine.

One of Davidson's brothers, 26-year-old Walter, was employed by the railways but at one time had been an apprentice machinist in Milwaukee. One day in 1902, while he was repairing a locomotive in Parsons, Kansas, a letter from Arthur invited him to drive the recently developed prototype with Harley. As he already had to go to Milwaukee to attend the wedding of the third brother in the family, William, Walter scheduled a test of the first Harley-Davidson. When he arrived, however, the bike was in pieces, as William and Arthur had counted on a specialist to finalize the bike. Captivated, Walter agreed to collaborate on the project in his spare time.

The initial prototype Harley-Davidson was finally completed in 1902, and in early spring 1903 it underwent its maiden road tests. That first motorcycle was built, like most bikes of the era, from a bicycle frame with a four-stroke single-cylinder engine, a pedal start-up and a direct transmission secured to the rear wheel via a belt. The engine, with a 24.74 cubic inch (405 cc) displacement and 3 x 3.5 inch (7.6 x 8.9 cm) bore and stroke, was not very impressive since you needed to pedal and because the overly sensitive bicycle frame often cracked.

16-17 THE 1912 MODELS HAD A LOWER DRIVING POSITION, AND THOSE OF THE "X" SERIES WERE EQUIPPED WITH A CLUTCH BUILT INTO THE REAR HUB.

At that time, companies like Indian, Thor and Wagner were already producing motorcycles, and Harley and Davidson decided to create bikes that were more in line with the standards of these manufacturers. Harley set out to design a more powerful engine with a larger displacement and a crankshaft that doubled in diameter, from 5 inches (13 cm) to 11.5 inches (29 cm). However, problems with the framework increased and they soon decided to abandon the bicycle frame and focus on producing their own framework, which would be inspired by what was considered the best at that time. With this strengthened and expanded motorcycle chassis, the engine placed in front of the pedals and, especially, with the new engine, the first Harley-Davidson prototype was finally born.

Two other bikes were built that year, bringing the total production of the Harley-Davidson Motor Company in 1903 to 3 motorcycles, which were sold in the summer and autumn for $200 each even before they were completed. The 1904 production of this single-cylinder motorcycle, called "Model 0," went from 4 to 8, and from 5 to 16 for 1905's "Model 1."

In 1913, the Harley-Davidson Company put out an advertising campaign announcing that one of these bikes had traveled 100,000 miles without problem. Originally acquired by a man named Meyer, it traveled 6,000 miles before reaching its second owner, George Lyon, who more than doubled Meyer's output, racking up 15,000 miles. Next, a Dr. Webster drove 18,000 miles and Louis Fluke put in 12,000 miles. Finally, the ultimate driver of this model, Stephen Sparrow, exceeded all previous owners, adding 32,000 miles.

18 PASSIONATE ABOUT FISHING, WILLIAM DAVIDSON AND WILLIAM HARLEY USED THEIR BIKES TO QUICKLY GET TO THEIR FAVORITE FISHING SPOTS, SUCH AS PINE LAKE IN HARTLAND, WISCONSIN.

19 THE MODELS PRODUCED AFTER THE FIRST HARLEY-DAVIDSON IN 1903 DID NOT UNDERGO ANY SIGNIFICANT CHANGES UNTIL 1906, AND THE OIL TANK REMAINED MOUNTED UNDER THE GAS TANK UNTIL 1908.

SINGLE CYLINDER F-HEAD (1906–1918)

The single-cylinder Harley-Davidsons with suction automotive inlet valves and leather drive belt remained the only motorcycles produced by the brand until 1909, when the first V-Twin Harley-Davidson appeared. These single-cylinder engine bikes were named F-head, and they would be manufactured until 1918.

In 1906, the Harley-Davidson Company had six full-time employees and produced 50 Model 2 machines featuring a new 27 cubic inch (440 cc) single-cylinder engine. In addition to the traditional black, it was available in an elegant Renault gray and was presented in this color on Harley-Davidson's first publicity flyers. It was soon nicknamed the "Silent Gray Fellow." This single-cylinder engine was also used in 1907 for 150 Category 3 Harley-Davidson bikes, which were equipped with a Springer fork newly acquired by William Harley at Sager, and the 450 Model 4s produced in 1908. In 1909 the single-cylinder gained 30 cubic inches (500 cc) and came in four models that were differentiated by battery, ignition and wheels – 26 inches (66 cm) or 28 inches (70 cm).

With 1122 single-cylinder engine Model 5s sold in 1909, the Harley-Davidson Motor Company truly emerged as a force in the domestic motorcycle market and would soon assert itself in both international markets and competition. The Model 6 of 1910 and Model 7 of 1911 remained virtually unchanged, but in 1912 the engine of the Model 8 benefited from a hand-operated oil pump, and models sporting an "X" in their name had a clutch built into the rear wheel hub which was operated by a lever located on the left side of the gas tank.

The range of single-cylinder Model 9 engines increased to 35 cubic inches (570 cc) in 1913. The model was named F-head and soon nicknamed "5-35," as the 35 cubic inches (570 cc) produced 5 horsepower. The semi-tumbled engine received

THE DESIGN OF THE HARLEY-DAVIDSON

was correct. That is why it has been so freely copied and why there was no necessity for our tearing it down and offering an experimental new model for 1909.

That's the only "Plus 5" Diamond Medal Winner

That's the Machine that made the World's Economy Record

The Performance of the Harley-Davidson

proved the correctness of the design and quickly placed it in the enviable position it occupies today. In every public competition which makes instructive comparison possible, the Harley-Davidson has acquitted itself handsomely and with high honors. It won the highest honors of 1908—the ONLY diamond medal and the ONLY "plus 5" perfect score in the F. A. M. national endurance contest, likewise first prize and a world's record in the national economy contest. A motorcycle of that sort ought to merit YOUR inquiry and consideration.

HARLEY-DAVIDSON MOTOR COMPANY, Milwaukee, Wis.

20 FOR 1909, HARLEY-DAVIDSON ANNOUNCED THAT, GIVEN THE PERFORMANCE AND SUCCESS OF ITS MOTORCYCLES, THE COMPANY WOULD NOT OFFER ANY NEW MODELS. THE COMPANY DECIDED INSTEAD TO IMPROVE AND MAINTAIN ITS ADVANTAGE OVER COMPETITORS AND IMITATORS.

20-21 WALTER DAVIDSON POSES WITH THE MODEL F-HEAD IN 1908. WITH IT HE WON AN ENDURANCE RACE ON LONG ISLAND, NEW YORK. IT WAS A PERFORMANCE THAT HELPED ESTABLISH THE REPUTATION OF HARLEY-DAVIDSON.

HARLEY-DAVIDSON

Special Qualities for use in War-time

STRENGTH   SPEED   SILENCE

are combined in the

HARLEY–DAVIDSON

The Perfection of Motor Cycle Combinations.

Send for "Honourable Mention" Brochure and Fully Illustrated 1916 Art Catalogue, post free. We invite your inquiries, which will be answered promptly

HARLEY-DAVIDSON MOTOR CO., LTD
Harleyson House, 74, Newman Street, London, W

THE SILENT GREY

22 While most people could not afford an automobile, motorcycles emerged as an economical means of transport. The addition of a sidecar allowed drivers to comfortably accommodate a passenger.

23 In 1916, the frame was reinforced and the bearings of the steering column were made larger so that the bike could better support a sidecar.

an automatic intake valve, and models were available with either a leather drive belt or chain drive. However, by 1914 sales of single-cylinder engines with a leather belt drive paled in comparison to models with a chain drive, and in 1915 the company abandoned the belt drive. All Models 10s were equipped with a clutch pedal, brake and step-starter. One model, the "C," possessed a two-speed gearbox incorporated in the rear hub.

Starting in 1916, the company used the last two digits of the year to designate the vintage of its models, and the Model 16 adopted the brand's

standard features, as the frame, brakes and steps were identical. On the "C" model, now equipped with a true three-speed gearbox, the pedal (the last vestige of bicycles) disappeared in favor of a real kick starter, while the model "B," which had only a single speed, conserved the pedal startup system.

On April 6, 1917, the United States declared war on Germany and nearly half of the 18,522 Harley-Davidsons produced that year, all painted khaki, were designated for the U.S. Army. In 1918, 26,708 motorcycles were manufactured

for both the military and civilian markets. Only 270 were single-cylinder engines, and by 1919, single-cylinder engines were no longer in the company catalog.

The single-cylinder engine would, however, make a return, most notably in 1921 and 1922, when a series was produced for commercial use. These were built on the base of a 74 cubic inch (1200 cc) V-Twin F-head engine with one cylinder removed. This single-cylinder 37 cubic inch (600 cc) retained the same chassis as the 74 cubic inch (1200 cc) V-Twin.

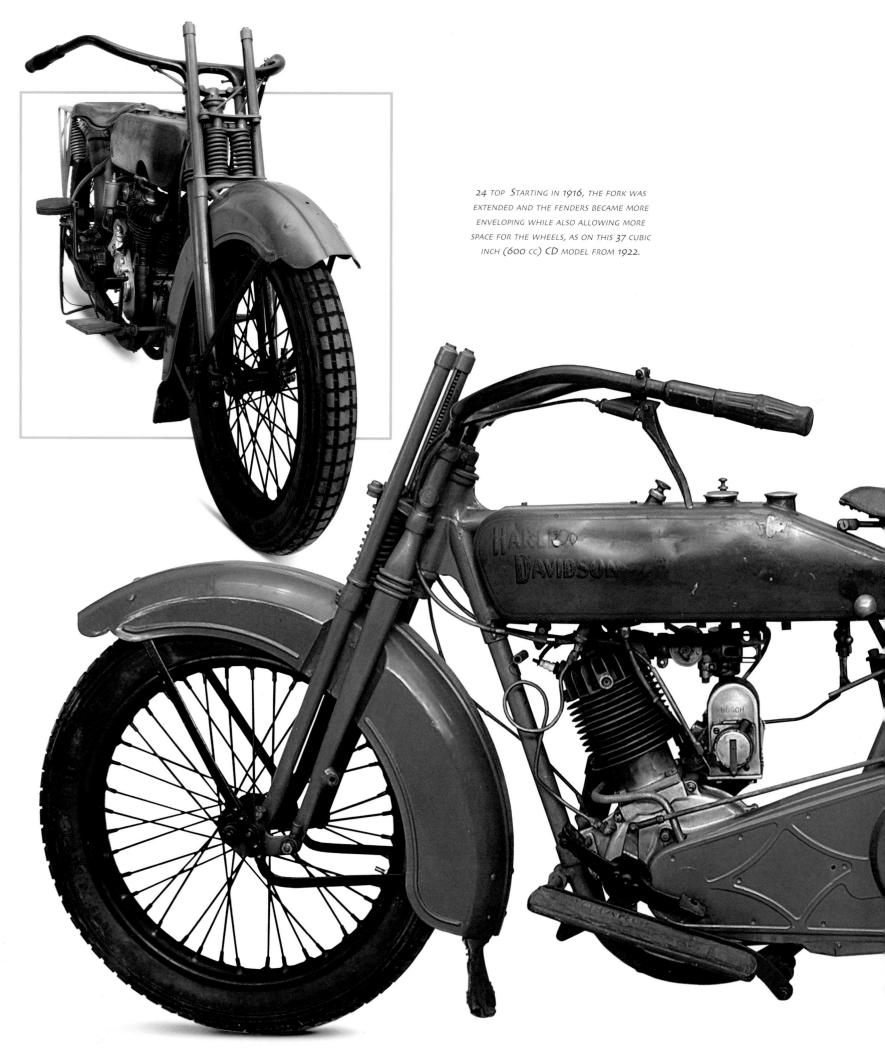

24 TOP *Starting in 1916, the fork was extended and the fenders became more enveloping while also allowing more space for the wheels, as on this 37 cubic inch (600 cc) CD model from 1922.*

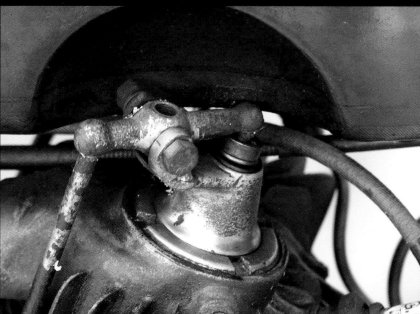

24-25 AND 25 IN 1921 AND 1922, THIS 37
CUBIC INCH (600 CC) CD, DESTINED FOR
COMMERCIAL USE, MAINTAINED THE CHASSIS
AND ENGINE ON MOTORCYCLES EQUIPPED WITH
THE 74 CUBIC INCH (1200 CC) V-TWIN F-74,
MEANING IT ALSO BENEFITED FROM NEW LIDS
FOR THE SPRING VALVES.

FLATHEAD OR OHV (1926–1934)

Single cylinder Harley-Davidsons returned to the brand's catalog in 1926 with two new 21 cubic inch (340 cc), 3-speed models equipped with Ricardo cylinder heads. Models "A" and "B" were powered by an engine with flat-head side valves, which preceded the similarly equipped V-Twin engine technology by three years and the V-Twin OHV Knucklehead "AA" and "BA" engines by 10 years. The S Racer over-head valve model, which possessed only one speed, was destined for competition.

These single-cylinder bikes were Harley-Davidson's answer to Indian's Prince single-cylinder. For this reason, there were many models – lateral distribution (flathead), overhead valve (OHV), magneto or battery ignition – and, most importantly, very attractive prices. The 21 cubic inch (340 cc) models were available for $210 for the A Solo (flathead and magneto), $235 for the B Solo (flathead and battery), $250 for the AA Sport Solo (OHV and magneto), $275 for the BA Sport Solo (OHV and drums) and $300 for the S Racer (OHV racing with magneto). This range of single-cylinder bikes was soon nicknamed "Peashooter," a name derived from the characteristic sound emitted by the bikes during competition. With a 21.09 displacement, the Peashooter quickly forged a formidable reputation for efficiency on the track. Including BAE AAE export models, sales of the Peashooters were very impressive, with 7990 single-cylinder models sold within the first year, a figure that put them on par with the 61 cubic inch (1000 cc) and 74 cubic inch (1200 cc) V-Twin engines, whose sales had totaled 14,285.

In 1927, Harley-Davidson added to its line of consumer bikes, producing a special series of single-cylinder engine motorcycles for competition. These served to promote the brand's image, as the SM OHV Racer, SA Racer and one-speed SMA Racer competed on the track. The A, AA and S Racer models were eventually also included in the category of bikes made especially for the 1928 competitive circuit. The B and BA models were given light alloy pistons and a lighter crankshaft, and they benefited from an extra front brake, an air filter and a throttle-controlled oil pump.

26 AND 27 TOP BEGINNING IN 1926, THE A AND B SIDE-VALVE MODELS, LIKE THIS 1928 VERSION, WERE PROPELLED BY THE SINGLE-CYLINDER FLATHEAD, WHILE BA AND AA MODELS WERE EQUIPPED WITH THE SINGLE-CYLINDER OHV ENGINE. BOTH MODELS WERE 21 CUBIC INCHES (350 CC), BUT THE MOTORCYCLES WITH THE FLATHEAD ENGINES SOLD BETTER.

27 BOTTOM THE 21 CUBIC INCH (350 CC) SINGLE-CYLINDER HARLEY-DAVIDSONS, SUCH AS THIS OHV ENGINE MODEL, BROUGHT THE BRAND MANY VICTORIES, WINNING WITH A CHARACTERISTIC SOUND THAT EARNED IT THE NICKNAME "THE PEASHOOTER."

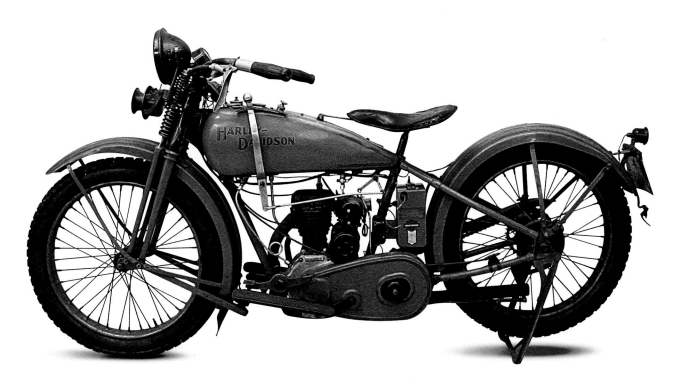

In 1929, the single-cylinder line was expanded with the arrival of the 30.50 cubic inch (500 cc) C Flathead, with side valves and battery. Robust and reliable, the block engine was mounted in the frame of the single-cylinder B21 model. In the wake of the economic crisis of 1929, many American motorcycle manufacturers disappeared.

When the dust settled, only Excelsior, Indian and Harley-Davidson remained.

To offset declining sales on American soil, Harley-Davidson had, by 1930, launched an aggressive international marketing campaign that allowed it to continue producing single-cylinder engine motorcycles. These bikes, however, would be mainly for export. That same year, the C 30.50 model adopted the framework of the V-Twin D 45 motorcycle and was released at the same time. It benefited from a lower seat height, improved ground clearance and superior handling. A magneto version, the 30.50 CM, was available on request.

In 1931, Harley-Davidson's only single-cylinder motorcycle was the C 30.50 model, which was now equipped with the same rear brake as the V-Twins. The A 21 models had disappeared from the catalog, and the B 21 and B models were for export only. Special versions of the 30.50 were also available by order, including the CH, CMG and CC. Further special editions were available in 1932, including the CC, CR and CS, and the company released these and the B 21 model in the U.S. market.

The BC 30.50 Flathead appeared the following year. The bike featured a single-cylinder engine mounted in a B 21 frame. Only one "special" model remained, the CS 30.50, which was reserved for the Japanese market. In 1934, the B 21, C 30.50 and CB 30.50 made up the company's entire line of single-cylinder bikes. They would become the last single cylinder bikes to appear in the Harley-Davidson catalog.

THE FIRST TWIN HARLEY-DAVIDSON, THE SPECIAL TWINS, AND THE F-HEAD BIG TWIN

V-Twin F-Head (1909, 1911–1929)
V-Twin Racer (1915–1921)
Flat-Twin W Sport Twin (1919–1923)
F-Head Big Twin (1921–1929)

THE FIRST TWIN V-TWIN F-HEAD (1909 AND 1911–1929)

In 1909, the 50 cubic inch (820 cc) 5-D model was the first Harley-Davidson powered by a V-Twin engine with cylinders positioned at 45 degrees, a particular alignment that would mark Harley-Davidson's place in motorcycle history. This engine was much anticipated, even though it largely relied on components of the excellent single-cylinder engine, with two connecting rods on the same crankpin. For this first year of production, 27 V-Twin bikes, featuring almost 7 horsepower and a 49.5 displacement, were built and sold for $325. Despite suction valves unsuited to the V-Twin and a belt drive that slipped due to a lack of tension, the bikes were relatively reliable. However, they soon began to encounter startup problems and were removed from the catalog at the end of the year.

In 1911, the V-Twin returned with the 49.5 cubic inch (820 cc) 7-D, which were called "50 cubic inch." It would become known as the F-head engine. The bike would undergo many changes and improvements and stay on the market until 1929. Boosting this success was the fact that it no longer suffered from the defects of the 1909 model and even had a reinforced frame. Its engine, equipped with inlet valves at the top that were controlled by a cam, was semi-tumbled. It featured 6.5 horsepower and a belt-tensioning device that helped remove the problematic slipping. The bike was a great success, with 5625 copies produced in 1911.

HARLEY-DAVIDSON MOTOR CYCLE

Model 5 "D"—7 H. P. Motor, Double Cylinder, Magneto Ignition only—Price $325.

The 8-D model of 1912, which had a new frame, was accompanied by the X-8-D clutch system, which was located in the hub of the rear wheel (free-wheel clutch), and the 61 cubic inch (1000 cc) X-8-E, with 8 horsepower and a chain drive.

In 1913, all V-Twins were 61 cubic inch (1000 cc) chain drives, 9-E and 9-F, and this engine was also used for a new vehicle, the Package Truck, or G Forecar Delivery Van, which was a commercial tricycle with a front-end trunk. Sales of V-Twins, not counting the G model, were very strong, with 6782 units sold. This exceeded the amount of single-cylinder engines bikes sold: 6111.

In 1914, all models were equipped with the step-start ignition system, with clutch and brake pedals. The 10-F model received a hub with a two-speed transmission, which disappeared in 1915 in favor of a real three-speed gearbox. This was also used for the 11-F (magneto ignition), 11-G Delivery Van, and 11-J (battery ignition system with electric lighting). Only the 11-E (magneto ignition) and 11-H (battery ignition system with electric lighting) retained a one-speed transmission. The 11-K model, developed by the competition department, experienced some reliability problems and remained at the prototype stage in 1915.

The Harley-Davidson magazine *The Enthusiast* appeared in 1916, and the company began using the year to name its motorcycles, which now benefited from a new standardization system. Frames, steps and brakes were identical on all models and, on three-speed machines, pedals, the last vestiges of bicycles, disappeared in favor of the kick starter. In spring of that year, Harley-Davidson was for the first time engaged in a military operation, which took place in northern Mexico against Pancho Villa.

On April 6, 1917, the United States declared war on Germany and nearly half of the 18,522

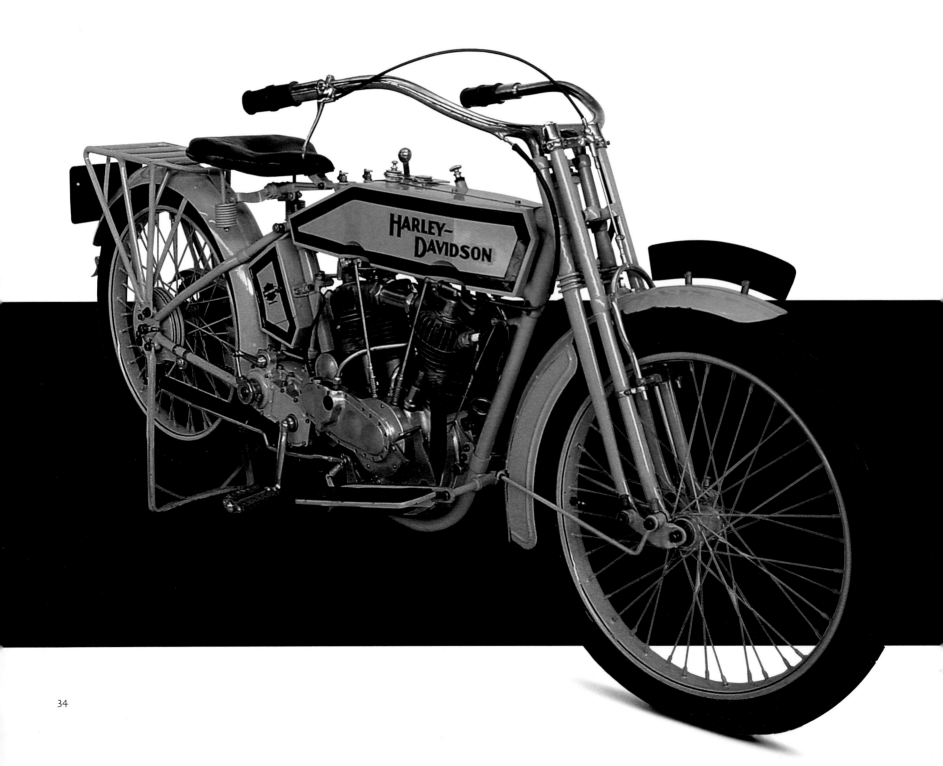

Harley-Davidsons produced that year were for the U.S. Army. In 1918, 26,708 motorcycles were produced for civilian and military markets, including 8,095 copies of the 61 cubic inch (1000 cc) 18-FUS model made uniquely for government use. In 1919, 23,279 were sold, as well as 7521 61 cubic inch (1000 cc) 19-FUS F-heads.

In 1919, the single-speed Model E was no longer in the catalog, which included the FS and JS ("S" for sidecar) in addition to the 61 cubic inch (1000 cc) F and J. A wide range of accessories and options were developed to transform and customize these bikes and, finding success with this formula, Harley-Davidson increased the list of components in subsequent years. This strategy touched all elements of their bikes, with special paint and nets, more comfortable saddles, wider fenders, different-sized tires and wheels, greater capacity gas tanks, different brake and clutch systems and many technical innovations gleaned from the competitive circuit. Apart from the adoption of a wider framework that lowered the seat height in 1925, this accessories policy allowed the 61 cubic inch (1000 cc) F-Head models to remain mostly unchanged until 1929.

The magneto ignition F Models were no longer in the catalog in 1926 and, in 1928, Harley-Davidson added a front brake. The new JH Two-Cam model, available in 1928 and 1929, had two camshafts operating the pushrod valves, different valve springs and larger fins for improved cooling. This latest innovation, derived from retired 61 cubic inch (1000 cc) F-Head competition models, offered higher performance.

34 THE THREE-SPEED TRANSMISSION
APPEARED ON THE HARLEY-DAVIDSON
11-F AND 11-J V-TWIN IN 1915.

35 THE PRIMARY DRIVE, CLUTCH,
GEARSHIFT LEVER AND FINAL
TRANSMISSION ON THE THREE-SPEED
MODELS WERE SITUATED ON THE SAME
SIDE OF THE BIKE.

36 *TOP LEFT* *STARTING IN 1916, THE STEERING COLUMN WAS REINFORCED AND ITS LARGER BEARINGS HAD TWO ADDITIONAL BALLS.*

36 *TOP RIGHT* *IN 1916, THE FORK WAS WIDENDED AS WERE THE FENDERS, WHICH WERE MOVED FARTHER AWAY FROM THE TIRES. THE HUB WAS GIVEN A FRONT FENDER, WHICH WAS ALSO ADOPTED ON EARLIER MODELS OF HARLEY-DAVIDSONS SO THAT THEY COULD BENEFIT FROM THESE IMPROVEMENTS.*

36-37 *THE CLUTCHES OF THE 1918 MODELS COULD BE LUBRICATED BY DRIVERS THANKS TO A RESERVOIR. THE FIRST CLUTCHES REQUIRED DISASSEMBLY AND LUBRICATION BY DEALERS.*

37 TOP IN 1918, THE AMERICAN MILITARY
SELECTED THE BEST ELEMENTS FROM EACH
MOTORCYCLE MANUFACTURER TO PRODUCE A
STANDARD BIKE. ALTHOUGH INDIAN PRODUCED
MOST OF THE 70,000 MOTORCYCLES USED BY
AMERICAN FORCES (HARLEY-DAVIDSON MADE
ONLY 20,000), THE ENGINE USED WAS A
HARLEY-DAVIDSON V-TWIN THAT WAS PLACED
WITHIN AN EXCELSIOR FRAMEWORK WITH AN
INDIAN FORK. THE PROJECT WAS ABANDONED
UPON THE END OF THE WAR.

38 AND 39 HARLEY-DAVIDSONS WERE AVAILABLE WITH AN OPTIONAL SIDECAR FOR ONE OR TWO PASSENGERS, OR FOR THE TRANSPORT OF GOODS IN A COMMERCIAL MODEL, WHICH COULD BE MOUNTED ON THE RIGHT OR LEFT SIDE OF THE BIKE. IT COULD ALSO BE DELIVERED, AS ANOTHER OPTION, WITH A SPECIAL SIDECAR ENGINE FROM 1916 TO 1918.

40 AND 41 *In 1923, the engine on the 61 cubic inch (1000 cc) 23J models had a new oil pump and its housings and lids were painted, while the nets decorating the fender and tank became three thin gold bands.*

42 AND 43 THE 1924 MODELS, LIKE THIS 24JE WITH NEW
ALUMINUM PISTONS, RECEIVED A FOUR-CELL BATTERY INSTEAD OF THE
THREE-CELL BATTERIES USED IN EARLIER MODELS. THIS NEW BATTERY
INCREASED THE BIKE'S CAPACITY BY 40 PERCENT. GENERATOR MODELS,
MEANWHILE, HAD LARGER BRUSHES AND ALTERED CONTACT ANGLES.

V-TWIN RACER (1915–1921)

Since 1912, the tumbled Indian V-Twins used in competitive racing featured four-valve cylinder heads, while the Excelsiors, another major American motorcycle manufacturer, used enormous valves. The battle on the professional circuit between the "Big Three" (Harley-Davidson, Indian and Excelsior) also reflected the commercial rivalry between these manufacturers, with Indian being the top American motorcycle maker in 1915.

In 1913, a Harley-Davidson racing department was finally created, and engineer William Ottaway was charged with creating a Harley-Davidson racing team. Thus, the Harley-Davidson eight-valve racing bike was developed in conjunction with English engineer Harry Ricardo, a specialist in combustion chambers. To participate in official competitions, the bike had to have a maximum displacement of 61 cubic inches (1000 cc) and be available commercially. Harley-Davidson based this bike on the configuration of its V-Twin 61 cubic inch (1000 cc) engine production model, the big difference being the adoption of cylinder heads, each with two intake valves and two exhaust valves. These were controlled by buttons and rockers from a single and unique camshaft positioned in the distribution crankcase.

This eight-valve engine was installed in a steel framework bolted to two steel plates that coated the motor crankcase. The base production racer model, equipped with a primary and secondary chain drive, had no gearbox or brakes, but multiple versions were produced for the different professional racing circuits. This meant that the bike came with different rockers and camshafts, with or without exhausts, with various forks, etc. Its hefty, prohibitive

$1,500 price tag, which was three times higher than other racing bikes, discouraged private bikers from purchasing them.

By 1916, a group of Harley-Davidson bikers, nicknamed the "Wrecking Crew," which included Jim Davis, Ralph Hepburn, Walter Cunningham and Leslie "Red" Parkhust, won many races, including 15 national championships. In 1921, the "Wrecking Crew" won all national competitions and broke speed records in the process. However, by the end of 1921 Harley-Davidson had abandoned competitive racing, as its sales had collapsed, mainly because of the availability of cars like the Ford Model T at prices only marginally higher than those of a motorcycle. This was a development that Harley-Davidson and Indian struggled to adapt to immediately.

44 The 1919 "W Sport-Twin," powered by a 36 cubic inch (600 cc) Flat-Twin engine, was a great bike but it lacked power and the allure of a V-Twin engine, which hurt its sales.

45 After World War I, motorcycle competitions resumed and Harley-Davidson dominated the circuit with "The Wrecking Crew" team at the helm of its fabulous racing motorcycles. The company's competition department, however, was suddenly closed at the end of 1921 following a decline in motorcycles sales.

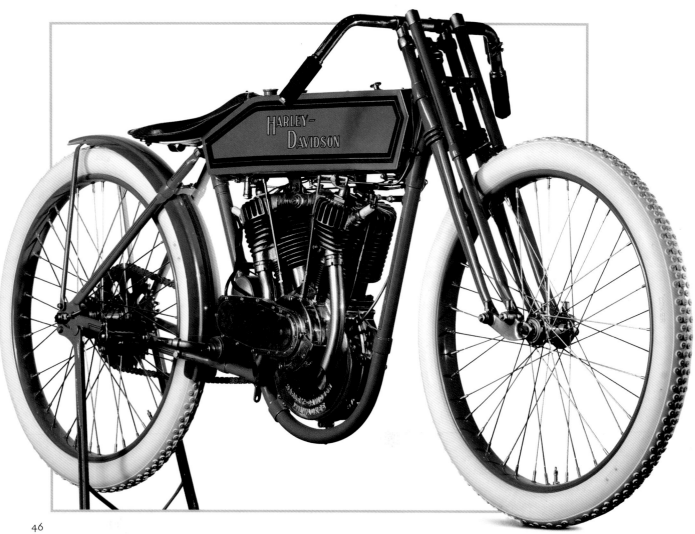

46 AND 47 *BEFORE THE EIGHT-VALVE V-TWIN RACER APPEARED IN 1916, HARLEY-DAVIDSON COMPETED WITH MODELS DERIVED FROM THE 1914 SERIES. THESE MOTORCYCLES, CALLED THE "K MODELS," WERE POWERED BY 61 CUBIC INCH (1000 CC) ENGINES BUILT BY THE FACTORY AND IDENTIFIED BY THE LETTER "M" ON THE SERIAL NUMBER.*

FLAT-TWIN W SPORT-TWIN (1919–1923)

After World War I, the motorcycle again became a vehicle of pleasure and innovations were needed to meet public expectations. Thus, in the middle of 1919, the new 35 cubic inch (580 cc) "W Sport-Twin" emerged, equipped with a longitudinal flat engine (Flat-Twin), with opposed cylinders and lateral distribution (Flathead). Inspired by the English manufacturer Douglas, it was presented as a lightweight sport bike. Technically, its innovations included a side-valve, a compact three-speed gearbox that was housed in the same casing as the engine and a secondary transmission, anchored above the engine block, that was controlled by a chain under the crankcase. Its primary transmission was ensured by gears in an oil bath, as was the clutch, and each head combined to form a single piece, which was the case for most bikes of the time. The motor was housed in a split crankcase and the bike's sophisticated fork suspension, which was also inspired by Douglas, provided excellent comfort even on poor surfaces.

However, this bike did not meet sales expectations in the U.S. market. Nevertheless, Harley-Davidson did not skimp on publicity and the "Sport-Twin" beat several endurance records. Still, with only 6 horsepower, it was more of a touring bike than a sport bike and its specifications did not appeal to Americans who preferred the V-Twin. It was no longer in the Harley-Davidson catalog in 1924.

48-49 STARTING IN 1920, THE V-TWIN RACER, LIKE THIS 1921 MODEL, WAS EQUIPPED WITH ENGINES DESIGNATED BY THE LETTER "E" AND THAT HAD ALUMINUM PISTONS. THERE WAS ALSO ANOTHER FRAME DIFFERENT THAN THE ONE SEEN IN THIS PHOTO, A SPECIAL MODEL RESERVED FOR DEALERS WHICH ALLOWED ONE TO REMOVE THE CYLINDERS WITHOUT REMOVING THE ENTIRE ENGINE FROM THE FRAME.

HARLEY–DAVIDSON

50 TOP AT THE END OF WORLD WAR I, THE EUROPEAN
MOTORCYCLE INDUSTRY WAS UNABLE TO SATISFY CUSTOMER
DEMAND AND HARLEY-DAVIDSON BENEFITED, EXPORTING ITS
MOTORCYLCES AND SIDECARS TO THE OLD WORLD AND IN THE
PROCESS PROVIDING TRANSPORTATION TO FAMILIES AT A LOWER
COST. HARLEY-DAVIDSON PRODUCED 16,095 SIDECARS IN 1919.

50-51 AND 51 TOP THE 1919 MODELS HAD THEIR HANDLEBARS
WIDENED BY 2.5 INCHES (6 CM) AND WERE THE LAST TO HAVE
THE HORN LOCATED ABOVE THE LIGHT. THEIR POSITIONS WERE
REVERSED STARTING IN 1920.

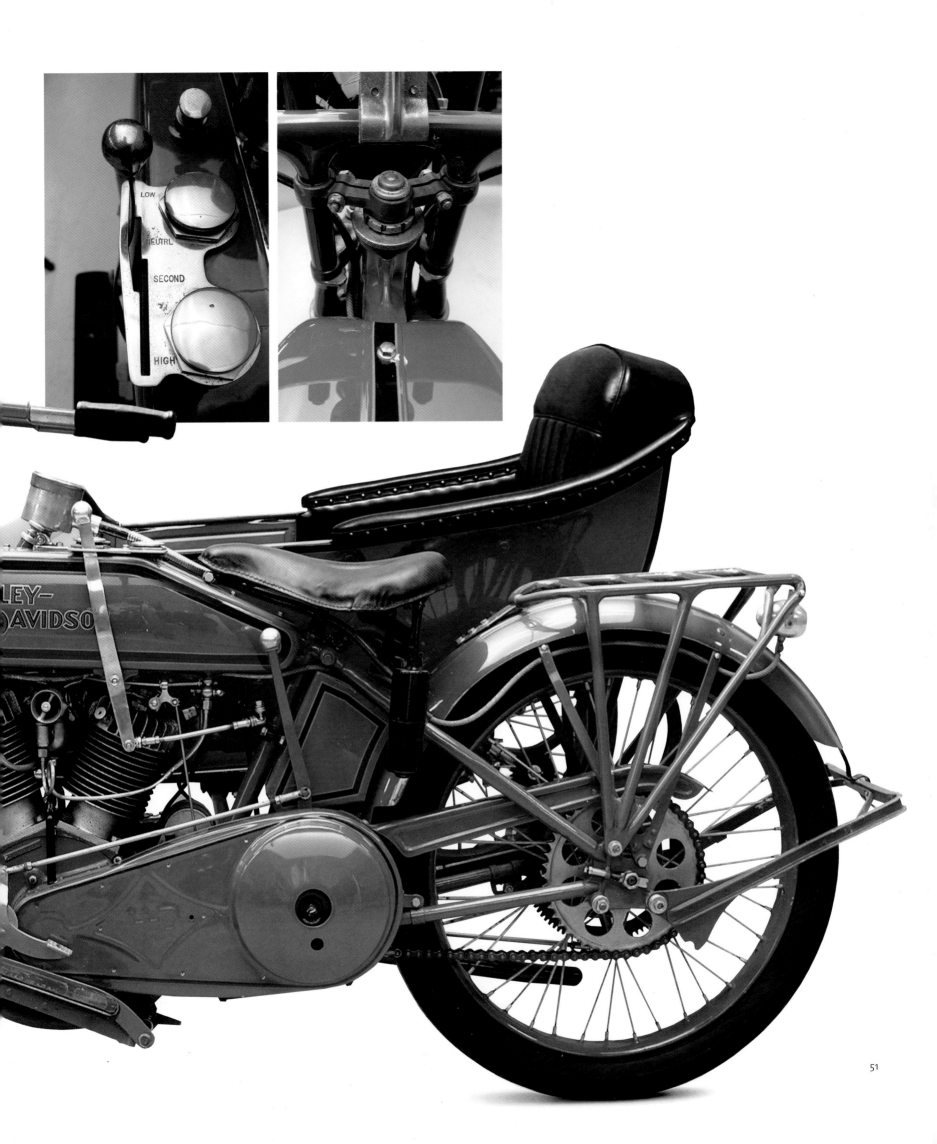

F-HEAD BIG TWIN (1921–1929)

After World War I, bikers were not only looking for powerful and reliable bikes, they wanted large and powerful engines, and Harley-Davidson had to meet this expectation. In 1921, 74 cubic inch (1200 cc) V-Twin engines appeared on the JD and FD models, which were still three-speed bikes. That same year, Harley-Davidson also released a 61 cubic inch (1000 cc) V-Twin and a W Sport Solo with a flat-twin engine.

These 74 cubic inch (1200 cc) bikes, however, were 61 cubic inch (1000 cc) models with the bore and stroke augmented to increase the displacement. In fact, they shared most of the 61 cubic inch's (1000 cc) characteristics. The FD 74 was equipped with a magneto ignition and the JD 74

had a battery ignition system with electric lighting. Models built for sidecars, designated by the letter "S" (FS, JS, FDS, JDS), had different compression rates and gear ratios. However, the 74 cubic inch (1200 cc) D series was considered the first true "Big Twin" Harley-Davidson.

In 1922, the olive green paint was replaced by a darker Brewster green, and the 74 cubic inch (1200 cc) benefited from some engine improvements in 1923 and 1924. But, in 1925, the adoption of a new, lower framework, with a different engine mounting system, made it possible to offer a lowered seat, greater comfort and a vastly improved driving position thanks to the extension of the saddle's spring in the central vertical tube of the frame. The 26-inch (65 cm) tires, which were 28 inches (70

cm) before, were widened and changed to the balloon variety, and the company began to seriously develop a range of accessories and options that let bikers transform and customize their bikes.

The magneto ignition F Models were no longer in the catalog in 1926 and, in 1928, Harley-Davidson added a front brake. The new JH Two-Cam model, known for high perfromance, was available in 1928 and 1929. It had two camshafts operating the pushrod valves, different valve springs and larger fins for improved cooling. However, this would be the end of the F-Head 74 cubic inch (1200 cc) motorcycle engine, as the new block D 45 Flathead engine made its first appearence in the 1929 catalog, and it was not confined to its initial 45.2 cubic inch (740 cc) displacement.

52-53 *The 1925 25JE model had a new chassis and teardrop tank, smaller 20 inch (50 cm) rims, a new taillight setting, an eccentric rear sprocket, an optional electrical control panel and many improvements that modernized Harley-Davidson. In 1925, the Harley-Davidson Big Twin received a cylindrical tool box mounted across the fork, as seen on this 25JE.*

53 *In 1925, the Harley-Davidson Big Twin was equipped for the first time with a new, wider frame that lowered the seat height, wheels and equipment, which was redesigned to emphasize the "streamline" aesthetic. It later received wider fenders in 1926.*

54 AND 55 *The 1928 28 JDS model with sidecar received, like other Harley-Davidsons of that year, a front brake. That same year, the Department of the Interior ordered 25 sidecars for National Park Rangers.*

56 AND 57 *The 1927 72 cubic inch (1180 cc) 27FD model was a special magneto ignition bike with aluminum pistons. The model in this photo was equipped with an optional luggage rack that came with added saddlebags.*

FLATHEAD

58-59 *The 45 WLD retained the same logos and designs while undergoing very few changes from 1941 to 1946, as Harley-Davidson focused on producing motorcycles for the United States Army.*

60 and 61 *In 1930, models of the Flathead D Series, which originally appeared in 1929, received a new framework that lowered the seat height, improved ground clearance and made the bike 100 percent stronger, at least according to the brochure used by dealers.*

1929–1951: 45 CI, D THEN R (1932), THEN WL (1937)

With the world economy on the verge of an historic crash, the new generation of Harley-Davidsons, the three-speed 45 cubic inch (740 cc) D Flathead, appeared in 1929. The chassis did not differ from previous models, but the design of this new engine would provide the basis for future Harley-Davidsons, with Flathead block engines of varying power propelling the bikes. The great stock market crash of October 1929 devastated the economy and, by year's end, there were only three U.S. motorcycle manufacturers: Harley-Davidson, Indian and Excelsior.

The 45 D side-valve V-Twin engine had about 18.5 hp and low compression for reliable touring use. The 45 LD, meanwhile, was a high compression sport version. These two bikes were equipped with a three-speed gearbox, a new 14-spring dry clutch, a kick starter, battery and ignition coils, and Ricardo cylinder heads. The models of 1929 and 1930 also had two headlights, which give them a unique aesthetic. The bikes' distinctive four-silencer exhaust system also contributed to their unique appeal.

By 1930, a new enhanced framework offered improved ground clearance, a lowered seat and easier access to the battery. The new bullet-shaped gas tank was larger and the round toolbox was attached to the fork in the headlights, while the exhaust system came with two silencers. The series was composed of the low compression D and DS (S for sidecar) models and the high compression LD and DLD Sport Special Sport, the latter being the model William H. Davidson Jr. used to win the 20th edition of the famous Jack Pine Endurance race. He finished with 997 points out of 1000.

The following year the models evolved, with a new Schebler Deluxe carburetor, frame reinforcements, a large headlight, the same rear brake as the old F-Head Big Twin and a single fishtail exhaust. But 1931 was the final year the 45 Flathead appeared under the R category of the Harley-Davidson catalog.

The R models (R Solo, RS Sidecar, RL Solo Sport and RLD Special Solo Sport) replaced the D line in 1932, with the same engine and a few significant improvements, including strengthened

62 and 63 In 1931, the Harley-Davidson catalog offered for the first time a choice of colors beyond the usual olive green, like on this 31 DL. The two-pipe exhaust was also replaced by a mono-tube Fishtail model.

valve springs, larger crankshafts, new engine cases, aluminum pistons, more efficient oil pumps, a horizontally fixed generator and a longer intake pipe equipped with a chrome air filter shaped like a hair dryer. The RLD sports model, meanwhile, received Linkert M11 or M16 carburetors. The framework also received other reinforcements, such as fork and fishtail exhausts, which were now 2.5 inches (6.5 cm) in diameter.

At the end of 1933, all 45 models were equipped with Linkert carburetors, and in 1934 they received a new oil pump, a new 12-spring clutch (which was easier to operate), a High-Flo exhaust and, to modernize their look, an Airflow taillight, fenders and a Solo Bucket saddle decorated with small rivets. During their last two years, 1935 and 1936, R models underwent few changes, such as a constant mesh transmission,

an improved air intake, cylinder fins with deeper grooves and a "Y" intake pipe.

In 1937, the W 45 Flathead series had adopted a similar design to the Knucklehead models and replaced the R 45. It came with a redesigned engine and a new oil system in which the pump was attached to the crankcase, against the gearbox. The left engine casing and distribution cover were decorated with horizontal ribs and the tank

64-65 AND 65 TOP LEFT IN 1932, THE 45 R SERIES, WHICH REPLACED THE STANDARD 45 D, BROUGHT MANY MECHANICAL IMPROVEMENTS TO THE 750 SIDE-VALVE, WHOSE NEW LINKERT CARBURETOR REPLACED THE SCHEBLER AND WAS ADORNED WITH AN ORIGINAL AIR FILTER.

was divided into two parts, the left for gas and the right for oil. The control panel was placed on the tank and consisted of a speedometer calibrated up to 120 mph (190 km/h), "White Face" Stewart-Warner dials with lights, an odometer and trip meter, a fuse box, an oil pressure gauge and an ammeter. The series included the high compression WL Solo Sport, the extra high compression WLD Special Sport Solo, the WLDR Competition Special (which was a racing model), the W Solo and the low compression WS Sidecar, plus a WSR model for the Japanese market.

Harley-Davidson equipped its W 45 series with a four-speed gearbox and a clutch similar to that of the Big Twin. While enhancing the aesthetic ties between the W 45 and the Big Twins, the company also replaced the oil pressure gauges and ammeter with lights in 1938 and continued to develop elements of the engine and chassis in 1939.

In 1940, the WLD and WLDR models received aluminum cylinder heads, reworked chambers, cylinder fins with deeper grooves and larger carburetors. Meanwhile, Babe Tancrede won the 200 Miles Expert Class C with a WLDR 45. The

footstools, shaped like a half-moon, replaced the older rectangular models, and even if more than 3500 law enforcement departments were now equipped with Harley-Davidsons, it was the U.S. Army that was the major beneficiary of these bikes. Harley-Davidson produced 36 copies of the 45 cubic inch (740 cc) WR Flathead Special, a racing bike derived from the 45 WLDR, in 1941, but military production monopolized the factory and sales of civilian motorcycles (affecting all Harley-Davidson models) dropped to about 6000 units, while 24,583 motorcycles were produced in all. On December 7 the Japanese attacked Pearl Harbor and on December 8 the Americans declared war on Japan, which was allied with Germany.

In 1942, Harley-Davidson mainly manufactured 45s – WLA for the U.S. Army and WLC for the Canadian military – while approximately 300 civilian WLD, WL and WLS models were made. There was no more production of Harley-Davidsons for the civil commercial market in 1943, but the U.S. federal government still authorized the provision of Harley-Davidsons for 137 American police forces. By February 1944 the military department had canceled an order for 11,331 bikes

and, on July 27, 450 motorcycles originally intended for military personnel were granted to the civilian market, followed by another 600 new machines on Sept. 8. From November 1944 the civilian production began offering optional aluminum cylinder heads for the 1945 four-speed 45 cubic inch (740 cc) WL model.

Besides the WL Solo 45, which was now a three-speed, and the WL-SP 45 with aluminum cylinder heads, which were produced until 1951, Harley-Davidson restarted production of the 45 cubic inch (740 cc) Flathead WR Racing in 1946, a bike that would be manufactured until 1952. Production grew again, although the U.S. government put up 15,000 WLA Army surplus for sale. The 1947 WL models received a "tombstone" rear light, a two-light dashboard painted the same color as the tanks, a black leather saddle and chrome elements that had disappeared during the war. And, in 1948, a side-car version of the WLS, produced until 1952, returned to the catalog. The W 45 models continued to receive new fenders, air filters, optional exhausts and other cosmetic changes and technical details until their disappearance from the Harley-Davidson catalog.

66 AND 67 STARTING IN 1937, THE W 45 REPLACED THE R 45. AS SEEN ON THIS 1938 38 WL, IT RECEIVED HORIZONTAL RIBS ON THE LID OF THE DISTRIBUTION AND A DASHBOARD WITH A SPEEDOMETER, WHICH WAS PLACED ON THE TANK.

68 AND 69 THE "DELUXE SOLO ACCESSORY GROUP" PACKAGE OF
THE 45 CUBIC INCH (740 CC) WL, WHICH WAS ALREADY WELL-
SUPPLIED WITH CHROME AND ACCESSORIES, RECEIVED CHROME
FENDERS, RUBBER PEDALS, A CHROME REARVIEW MIRROR, A
CHROME PARKING SIDELIGHT AND CHROME LEG GUARDS.

70 AND 71 *STARTING IN 1940, THE WLD AND WLDR WERE CHARACTERIZED BY THE ADOPTION OF ALUMINUM CYLINDER HEADS AND COOLING FANS WITH DEEPER GROOVES. THEY ALSO RECEIVED A BIGGER CARBURETOR.*

74 V AND U (1930–1948) AND 80 V AND U (1935–1941)

In 1930, the 61 cubic inch (1000 cc) would temporarily disappear from the Harley-Davidson catalog and the 74 cubic inch (1200 cc) side-valve Flathead engines, controlled by a cam and equipped with three-speed gearboxes, replaced the 74 cubic inch (1200 cc) F-Head and Two-Cam. This mechanical revolution was expected following the appearance of the 45 cubic inch (740 cc) Flathead engine in 1929. Low compression models, like the V Solo and VS Sidecar, had Ricardo cylinder heads and magnesium alloy pistons, just like the high compression VL and VC Solo Sport Commercial models. The reinforced frames, which were 25 percent heavier than the models they replaced, were equipped with rectangular foldable steps, an ignition with two independent coils and a dual exhaust system on the right side of the bike. In addition to the four models in the 74 cubic inch (1200 cc) V Flathead line, special magneto models, the VMS Sidecar, the high compression VLM and the VMG were produced in small quantities in 1930 and 1931.

All of the 1931 V Big Twins were equipped with a new Schebler Deluxe carburetor which replaced the dual exhaust mufflers with a single Fishtail and, from the middle of the year, they were available with a reverse option for models with side-cars. The four V 74 cubic inch (1200 cc) models received some minor improvements in 1932, including larger generator brushes, which provided smoother current and overall bike operation.

In 1933, in addition to the four standard models – the V, VS, VL and VC, which were available with a choice of aluminum or magnesium alloy pistons – the VLD Special Sport Solo appeared, complete with high compression magnesium alloy pistons. Special models – the VF Solo and VFS Sidecar – were equipped with nickel-iron alloy pistons, and the entire line of V 74 cubic inch (1200 cc) models adopted a "Linkert" carburetor before the end of 1933.

In 1934, this line of 74 cubic inch (1200 cc) V-Twins consisted of the high compression VLD Special Sport Solo, low compression Solo VD, low compression VDS Sidecar, VFD Sidecar with nickel-iron alloy pistons and VFD Solo with nickel-iron alloy pistons. These bikes were equipped with a "High-Flo" exhaust, an "Airflow" taillight, larger fenders and a "Solo Bucket" saddle decorated with small rivets that helped modernize the look of the bike.

72 AND 73 IN 1930, THE FLATHEAD V SERIES MODELS, LIKE THIS
74 CUBIC INCH (1200 CC) VL 74, REPLACED THE J AND JD
MODELS WITH F-HEAD ENGINES. THEY WERE GIVEN REMOVABLE
RICARDO HEADS FOR EASY ACCESS TO VALVES AND PISTONS. THE
TWO LIGHTS WOULD BE REPLACED BY A SINGLE MODEL IN 1931.

Harley-Davidson would soon copy automakers who had adopted an Art Deco style, which emphasized bright and contrasting hues to lure customers during this difficult economic period.

The largest Harley-Davidson engine, the new 80 cubic inch (1300 cc) Flathead, which was built on the base of the 74 cubic inch (1200 cc) side-valve V-Twin Flathead and whose bore and stroke had been increased, arrived in late 1935. Because of this delay, it did not appear in the company's advertising brochures, as the new Knucklehead engine garnered most of the attention. This engine, which was housed in the same chassis as the 74 cubic inch (1200 cc), powered the 80 cubic inch (1300 cc) VLDD Sport Solo, the VDDS Sidecar and the family of 74 cubic inch (1200 cc) bikes: the VLD Special Sport Solo, VD Solo, VDS Sidecar, VLDJ Competition Special and VFD Solo.

The 80 cubic inch (1300 cc) engines outfitted the VLH Sport Solo and VHS Sidecar and were available, like the V 74 cubic inch (1200 cc), in VF versions with nickel-iron alloy pistons in 1936. The 74 cubic inch (1200 cc) VMG, meanwhile, came with a magneto ignition. The grooves of the cylinder fins and cylinder heads were made deeper that year, and the new design of the combustion chambers allowed for slightly better performance, which could be exploited even more with an optional four-speed gearbox.

The line of 74 cubic inch (1200 cc) and 80 cubic inch (1300 cc) Flathead engines became the U-74 and UH 80 in 1937. The engines benefited from a redesigned oil system and adopted many items from the 1936 E 61 cubic inch (1000 cc) Knucklehead models, including a four-speed gearbox, clutch, transmission, frame and a separate oil tank under the saddle and behind the engine and suspension. The equipment and general aesthetics were also similar, with the tank divided into two parts that supported the dashboard, which included a speedometer calibrated up to 120 mph (190 km/h), "White Face" Stewart-Warner dials, lights, odometer, trip odometer, fuse box, oil pressure gauge and ammeter. The 74 cubic inch (1200 cc) UMG magneto model and the 74 cubic inch (1200 cc) UL Special Sport Solo, Solo U and US Sidecar models were turned into 80 cubic inch (1300 cc) bikes and renamed ULH, UH and UHS, with few other changes, for the years 1938, 1939 and 1940.

The fender light, which appeared in 1938, was a "standard accessory." This light was an option for all models, and future Harley-Davidson owners were soon determining the finish of their bikes with an array of options. Similarly, all Harley-Davidson models soon adopted the famous "cat's eye" dashboard (so named because of its shape) on the tank, the "Boattail" taillight in place of the old "Beehive" and steps in the shape of a half moon in 1940.

In 1941, the last year of the 80 cubic inch (1300 cc) UH models, all the Flathead U 74 and UH 80 models, except the UMG 74 Magneto (which was no longer available), adopted a frame with a different caster angle and a new clutch. However, innovations were limited due to the fact that production was now oriented primarily for the military. The three 74 cubic inch (1200 cc) models – the 1942 UL, U and US – had to wait until 1945 for optional aluminum cylinder heads. In 1946 they changed their caster angle and adopted the "Tombstone" taillight in 1947 and the new "Wishbone" framework in 1948, the last year of production.

74 AND 75 THE MOTORCYCLES WITH 74 CUBIC INCH (1200 CC) AND 80 CUBIC INCH (1300 CC) FLATHEAD ENGINES (LIKE THIS 74 CUBIC INCH [1200 CC] D), WHICH WERE PART OF THE V-SERIES UNTIL 1936, BECAME THE 74 CUBIC INCH (1200 CC) U AND 80 CUBIC INCH (1300 CC) UH MODELS IN 1937, WHEN THEY ENJOYED A REDESIGNED OIL SYSTEM AND THE KNUCKLEHEAD ENGINE.

KNUCKLEHEAD

In 1936, the highly anticipated E and EL 61 V-Twin models with overhead valves finally made their apperance. Not only was this engine a real novelty, its style was also revolutionary and unique for Harley-Davidson. This was the brand's first twin series powered by a single camshaft via pushrods.

Tests on this engine dated back to the economic crisis that led to the Great Depression. On March 31, 1931, Excelsior-Henderson ceased business, leaving only Indian and Harley-Davidson in the American market. Harley-Davidson, however, was barely hanging on, operating at only 10 percent of its production capacity. It had, in fact, lost $17,000, with only 10,407 bikes produced. The era encouraged cost reductions, but Harley-Davidson management decided to invest in new machinery and production in order to reinvigorate sales, beginning with a study on a 61 cubic inch (1000 cc) tumbled V-Twin in the winter of 1931–1932. Its production was launched in 1935 for the appearance of the first 61 cubic inch (1000 cc) E OHV Knucklehead in 1936. It was unveiled during the annual Harley-Davidson dealer convention on November 25, 1935, at the Hotel Schroeder in Milwaukee. This was a year too early, according to driver Joe Petrali, who was working with the team in developing the engine and

who would have liked to finish a series of tests in order to correct defects and an ongoing oil leak problem. But Harley-Davidson, its dealers and especially its customers were anxiously awaiting this revolutionary new 61 cubic inch (1000 cc) bike, which boasted roughly 10 horsepower more than the heavy 74 cubic inch (1200 cc) Flathead motorcycles.

This bike, powered by the new 61 OHV (Overhead Valves) was the first Harley-Davidson production model that truly innovated in all areas, laying the foundation for all modern Harley-Davidsons. It was equipped with the first mass-produced Harley-Davidson double-cradle frame and a Springer fork reinforced with molybdenum steel. The bike featured closed-circuit lubrication with a dry crankcase and a separate U-shaped oil tank fixed to the frame under the seat and behind the engine. The improved oil pump had a controlled rate that depended on engine speed to ensure the maintenance of adequate pressure when the engine was running at low revs. The distribution of valves was done by four individual cams mounted on a central camshaft and rockers controlled by rods. The nickname "Knucklehead" would soon be bestowed on this unique bike due to its bone-shaped rocker covers. The transmission, meanwhile, had four gears and

76-77 THE OHV (OVERHEAD VALVE) KNUCKLEHEAD ENGINE, AVAILABLE IN THE 61 CUBIC INCH (1000 CC) E SERIES FROM 1936 TO 1947, OFFERED SIGNIFICANTLY MORE POWER THAN MODELS WITH SIDE VALVES. THE 1937 MODEL ALSO HAD A FILTER COVER THAT LOOKED DIFFERENT FROM THAT OF THE 1936 BIKE.

78-79 THE KNUCKLEHEAD DASHBOARD, WITH A SWITCH, SPEEDOMETER, INDICATORS AND MECHANICAL OIL PRESSURE AND AMMETER, WAS A FIRST FOR HARLEY-DAVIDSON. IN 1936 THE COUNTER WAS SCALED UP TO 100 MILES (160 KM), THEN UP TO 120 MILES (190 KM) IN 1937.

a disc clutch whose friction point had been greatly increased to facilitate shifting and to provide a smoother ride, one enhanced by the sound of the fishtail exhaust. In addition, its new streamlined aesthetic won the support of dealers and riders and fit in with the popular Art Deco style of the time. The dashboard, which was now mounted on the tank, was another innovation, with a speedometer, contactor and mechanical indicators for oil pressure and ammeter. However, the bike still had 18-inch (45 cm) wheels, just like the 45 (740 cc), 74 (1200 cc) and 80 cubic inch (1300 cc) Harley-Davidson Flatheads.

During this first year of marketing, the frame was reinforced and other enhancements corrected some early teething problems. The Knucklehead was attractive in appearance and performance, and in that first year 1704 copies would be produced in medium compression E Solo, high compression EL Special Sport Solo and medium compression ES Sidecar versions.

The framework, which had already been strengthened, was further reinforced, given anchors for a side-car in 1937 and a larger rear brake. The stick shift was changed and the selection grill attached to the side of the tank. It now had notches for locking the stick shift, even when in neutral. The Stewart-Warner meter went from a 100 mph (160 km/h) maximum to 120 mph (190 km/h), but the big news that year for the Knucklehead came in sports. Joe Petrali, who also won the 1937 hill-climbing championship, set a speed record while riding the Streamliner 61 OHV on Daytona Beach. His dual carburetor EL model set a world speed record of 136.183 mph (220 km/h).

While the E Solo disappeared in 1938, the transmission and braking system were improved and the rocker arms tightly enclosed under the

cover of pressed steel. Partially open before, they now emitted fumes of dirty oil, which caused some riders to complain. Lighted dashboard indicators, meanwhile, replaced the mechanical oil pressure and ammeter of the first Knuckleheads.

In 1939, the Knucklehead benefited from many small mechanical changes, especially to the pistons and oil pump, which improved reliability. The dash cover, which housed the dashbord on the tank, adopted a more fluid and profiled shape and its style was dubbed "cat's eye." Meanwhile, the new rear boat taillight, which replaced the old beehive model, was painted the same color as the mudguards. While an optional three-speed transmission with a reverse gear appeared, Harley-Davidson changed the position of

its gear ratios. In 1939, only neutral was situated between second and third. Likewise, the leather of the seat went from black to brown, a change that would also disappear by 1940.

The year 1940 proved to be significant for the Knucklehead, as it benefited from many improvements to the pistons, connecting rods, the size of the crankpin and an extension of its intake pipes in the cylinder heads. This was a modification that was related to the adoption of a larger, 1.5 inch (4 cm) Linkert carburetor. There were also numerous aesthetic changes, such as the cover of the distribution housing now donning eight fins and the adoption of half-moon steps. Note that in 1940 Harley-Davidson motorcycles could be equipped with optional 16-inch (40 cm) rims.

The big news in 1941 was the appearance of the 74 cubic inch (1200 cc) F Knucklehead which, alongside the E 61, completed an entire line of Knuckleheads, including the high compression 61 cubic inch (1000 cc) El and 74 cubic inch (1200 cc) FL Special Sport Solo and the medium compression 61 cubic inch (1000 cc) ES and 74 cubic inch (1200 cc) FS sidecar. To turn the 61 cubic inch (1000 cc) to 74 cubic inches (1200 cc), the bore and stroke were increased and the crankshaft gained weight and diameter. The 61 cubic inch (1000 cc) and 74 cubic inch (1200 cc) models also benefited from new crankcases, clutch and exhaust, a new 29 degree caster angle and an aircraft-styled finish. From 1941 on, all Harley-Davidsons came with 16-inch (40 cm) wheels.

But, on December 7, the Japanese attacked Pearl Harbor and, on December 8, the Americans declared war on Japan. Harley-Davidson's priority was no longer evolving the style of civilian bikes. The 1942 models retained the colors of the 1941 line and the oil pump was painted white, since the metal required to manufacture aluminum paint was rationed. The Knucklehead line from 1941, 1942 and 1943 were comprised of the high compression 61 cubic inch (1000 cc) EL and 74 cubic inch (1200 cc) FL Special Sport Solo and the medium compression 61 cubic inch (1000 cc) E and 74 cubic inch (1200) F Solo.

Rationing was increased in 1943 and the metal acronyms on the tank were no longer chrome but painted gray, black or blue with red lettering and spikes in black or cream. The mudguards no longer had wheel covers, the air filters were painted black, the front fender light was removed, footsteps were made of streaked plate, the seats were upholstered in horsehair and the only available color was gray. In 1944, because of the lack of raw materials, the tires of motorcycles were S-3 models made out of synthetic rubber, and the body of the Linkert carburetors were painted black due to a lack of silver paint. The ES and FS Sidecar models returned to the catalog as special models during that year, and sidecar models were once again incorporated into the catalog the following year.

In 1946, things slowly returned to normal and, by the end of the year, the models that featured a new framework caster angle of 30 degrees again received aluminum paint for mechanical parts in addition to chrome parts, seats cushioned with latex foam, a fork with an optional shock instead of ride control friction and a new Springer offset fork towards the front.

The last year of production for the Knucklehead, 1947, was a record year, as 11,648 models came off the assembly lines. Gear selection was inverted, with first gear being at the back now and not in front, for an alignment that looked like this: 1-N-2-3-4. A tombstone taillight replaced the boat tail, while a two-light dashboard, painted the color of the tanks, replaced the cat eye. These last Knuckleheads were also outfitted with a black leather seat and featured the chrome that had disappeared during the last war. These engines would soon give way to the panhead engine in 1948.

82 *The 1938 Knucklehead had graphics on the tank and was customizable, which transformed it into a traditionally-styled Harley-Davidson with more "modern" accessories issued from the brand's catalog, such as the seat and the windshield.*

83 *The 74 cubic inch (1200 cc) Knucklehead F Series, which appeared in 1941, did not achieve the success it deserved because of the war, which disrupted production.*

84 The console of the dashboard, attached to the tank, was new for 1947. Its shape was modernized and called "two-light," but it was still painted the color of the tank, with chrome an option. The speedometer now featured red needles, large, easy to read numbers and a gradient background that went from black on the exterior to white at the center. On this model, which used kilometers, the bottom of the meter remained the "airplane" (aviation) model used since 1941.

85 The 1947 EL Knuckelhead model brought back chrome elements, adopted a new type of "tombstone" taillight and reversed the order of gears in the tank. It was the last year of the Knucklehead.

MILITARY HARLEY-DAVIDSON

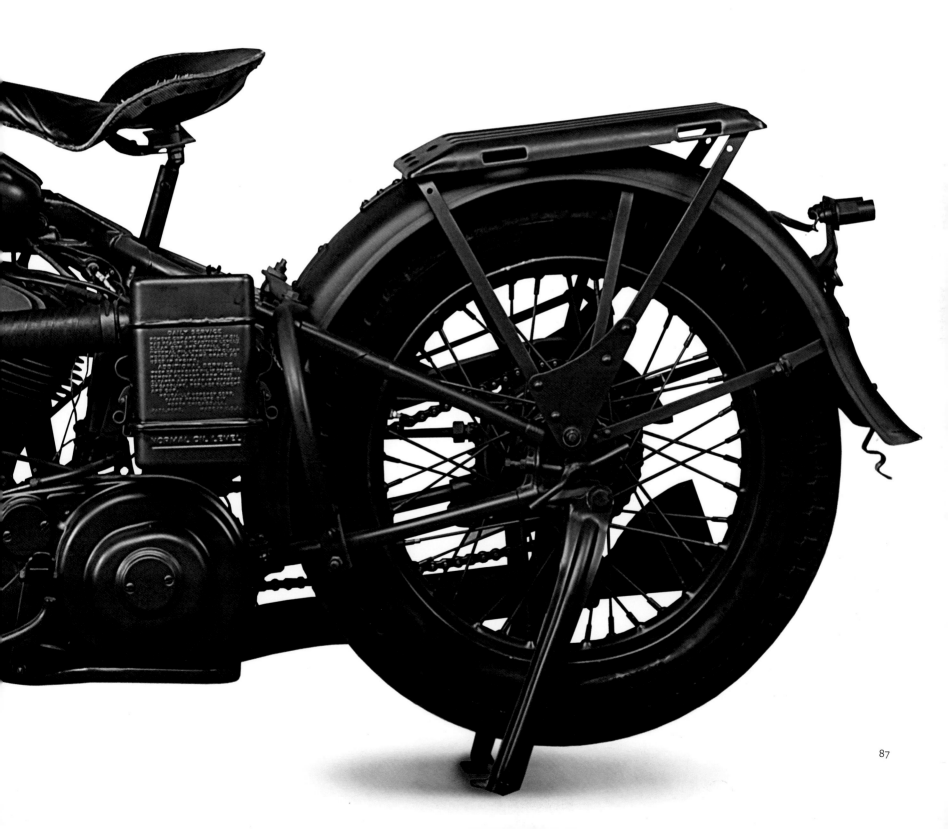

750 WLA (1940–1945)

In 1939 Harley-Davidson had sent motorcycles to be tested at a military base in Kentucky at the request of the Army. The military began resistance testing for both Harley-Davidson and Indian motorcycles at training camps. At the same time, many other specific tests were undertaken by Harley-Davidson on its own test tracks. Fittingly, these experimental motorcycles evolved according to the specifications of the Army, which was an expensive but effective way of operating since it led to the development of a first class military Harley-Davidson, the famed WLA.

In 1940, the WLD and WLDR models were equipped with aluminum cylinder heads. More than 3500 law enforcement forces were equipped with Harley-Davidsons, but the U.S. military was now the main beneficiary of these bikes. The Army placed an initial order of 745 WLAs, the militarized version of the WL, then 185 WLA and 74 cubic inch (1200 cc) Flatheads, for a total production of 10,461 motorcycles. The WL Army model was powered by a side-valve V-Twin whose compression ratio was lowered so that the heavy machine could still be effective at very low speed. The WLA engine, now equipped with aluminum heads, tolerated high temperatures, and its Linkert carburetor received a large oil bath air filter. The chassis was strengthened and equipped with military accessories which increased its weight, including two cylinder guards, a steel plate under the protective framework, various additional fasteners that would allow the fixing of arms and other military elements, a large steel rack and, to accommodate a rifle or machine gun, a leather sheath attached along the fork that could be reached by the driver.

In 1941, military production monopolized factory output and sales, and civilian sales dropped to about 6000 units out of 24,583 motorcycles produced in all. The Japanese attacked Pearl Harbor, and on December 8 the Americans declared war on Japan. In 1942, Harley-Davidson produced the

86-87 The "WL Army" model, powered by the V-Twin 45 cubic inch (740 cc) side valve and destined for the U.S. military, came in WLA and WLC versions for the Canadian Army.

88 and 88-89 Before this bike was retained by the Army, it underwent numerous tests to determine necessary improvements. The WLA 45 would eventually receive significant changes compared to the civilian model.

WLA for the U.S. Army and WLC for the Canadian Army (the "C" stood for Canada). The latter, unlike the WLA, was equipped with a manual clutch and a front brake taken from the Big Twin. Amid all of these large-scale war preparations, Harley-Davidson was forced to abandon the civilian motorcycle market. In addition to the WLA, Harley-Davidson assembled some 74 cubic inch (1200 cc) Flathead Big Twins for the U.S. Army and 45 copies of the 61 cubic inch (1000 cc) ELC Knucklehead for the Canadian Army.

Production for the U.S. Army continued to minimize production for the civilian market from 1941 to 1945, so much so that in 1943 there were no longer Harley-Davidsons manufactured for the civil commercial market. The U.S. federal government, however, still authorized the provision of Harley-Davidsons to 137 U.S. police forces.

At that time, it was difficult to purchase a Harley-Davidson in a private capacity. You had to first obtain a procurement card available at public agencies that had the authority to issue them. This process was rarely successful for the applicant, however, since the majority of exemptions were only granted on the grounds of national defense.

The standard color for all new civilian machines was now gray, and at American dealers a general depression set in. Civilian demand still existed, but the Second World War meant that the priority was always supplying the war effort.

In recognition of its merits and patriotic services rendered, Harley-Davidson received the prestigious E Army-Navy award ("E" for "excellence") in a ceremony on May 12, 1943. But in February 1944 the military department canceled an order for 11,331 bikes, forcing Harley-Davidson to lay off 500 employees. During the summer of 1945, the company reduced its workweek. On June 6, the Allies landed in Normandy, and on July 27 450 motorcycles originally intended for the military were put on the civilian market, followed by 600 more new machines on September 8. That year, production totaled 18,688 motorcycles.

The victory over the Nazis was celebrated on May 8, 1945, and the surrender of Japan on August 14. During World War II, Harley-Davidson had delivered more than 88,000 WLA military models and 20,000 WLC, with enough spare parts to build 30,000 more. The U.S. government began selling its surplus to the public before the end of 1945. In November, production of civilian motorcycles offered optional aluminum heads on the WL 45 and U 74 cubic inch (1200 cc) models, and the company gradually returned to the level of civilian production from years past.

90 AND 91 THE AIR FILTER OF THE *WLA* WAS AN OIL BATH MODEL WITHIN THE LATERAL HOUSING, AND THE FRONT FORK WAS USED TO SUPPORT THE BOX OF AMMUNITION AND THE WEAPON THAT WAS SO HANDY TO THE DRIVER.

92 AND 92-93 THE LIGHT OF THE WLA WAS MOVED LOWER TO PROTECT IT IN THE EVENT OF A FALL, AND THE ORIGINAL AXES OF THE WHEELS WERE REPLACED BY AXES THAT COULD BE REMOVED BY PULLING ON THEM WITHOUT HAVING TO HIT THEM.

AMMUNITION ONLY

750 XA (1942–1943)
1942–1943: 45 CI XA (FLATHEAD FLAT TWIN)

While the United States was not yet at war, the U.S. military was beginning to make preparations. It had been very impressed by the performance of the BMWs and Zundapps in North Africa, and so it asked Indian and Harley-Davidson to design a similar motorcycle, one that could match the performance of its German counterparts. Like the German models, these motorcycles had to be equipped with a Cardan, or drive shaft, since the chain would not hold up on sandy soil.

The chief of staff of the U.S. military met the manufacturers in February 1941 and negotiated an order for 1000 Harley-Davidson motorcycles to be delivered in July 1942. Harley-Davidson management purchased a military BMW R 12 model and produced a replica called the XA. The motorcycle had a drive shaft which could stand up to sand and was powered by a 45 cubic inch (740 cc) transverse side-valve flat-twin engine, a configuration that had the advantage of offering better cooling in the desert. Distribution was ensured by a camshaft located in the engine casing, the lubrication system was based on a wet sump design and two carburetors fed the cylinders. The fork was not the telescopic German variety but instead the Springer fork that equipped the Knucklehead models, and the bike featured a foot-operated transmission.

From December 1941 to February 1942 trials and tests of the XA were conducted at Camp Holabird, with the Army yet to make its final decision. Before it could do so, it needed the 1000 ordered bikes to be delivered and tested, since the XA Harley-Davidson continued to face competition from the Indian 841 model, which had a transverse V-Twin engine, like the current Moto-Guzzi, and a drive shaft. In mid-1942, all XAs were delivered and Harley-Davidson began researching and developing a sidecar with a driving wheel for the XA. Only three models with this sidecar driving wheel, dubbed "XS," would be built, as they never passed the experimental prototype stage.

In early 1943, Harley-Davidson seemed to have won the competition against Indian by promising a shorter delivery time for an eventual order of 25,000 drive shaft bikes. But on July 3 the military department told Harley-Davidson that the XA was no longer part of its acquisition plans, with the WLA 45 cubic inch (740 cc) becoming the only military motorcycle. Meanwhile, the Jeep had established its outstanding ability in all terrains, and the 1011 copies of the XA that were already assembled would never see the battlefield. Harley-Davidson then began to consider various possible civilian versions of this bike. One version, featuring an OHV engine (dubbed "XOD"), was being worked on in October 1944 when the Air Force appeared interested in the engine. The Air Force ordered 4975 XOD engines to serve as generators. However, after the victory over Japan in August 1945, military contracts were canceled and none of these XOD engines were ever fully assembled.

At the end of 1945, a sport bike and a Servi-Car powered by an XA motor were being developed for future Harley-Davidson production. However, these projects never made it to the next step in production as Harley-Davidson had other priorities, the most pressing being the development of an updated version of its V-Twin engine. The Army would eventually sell off its surplus XA military motorcycles on the civilian market, and about 200 XA models were transformed into civilian bikes that were much sought after by collectors.

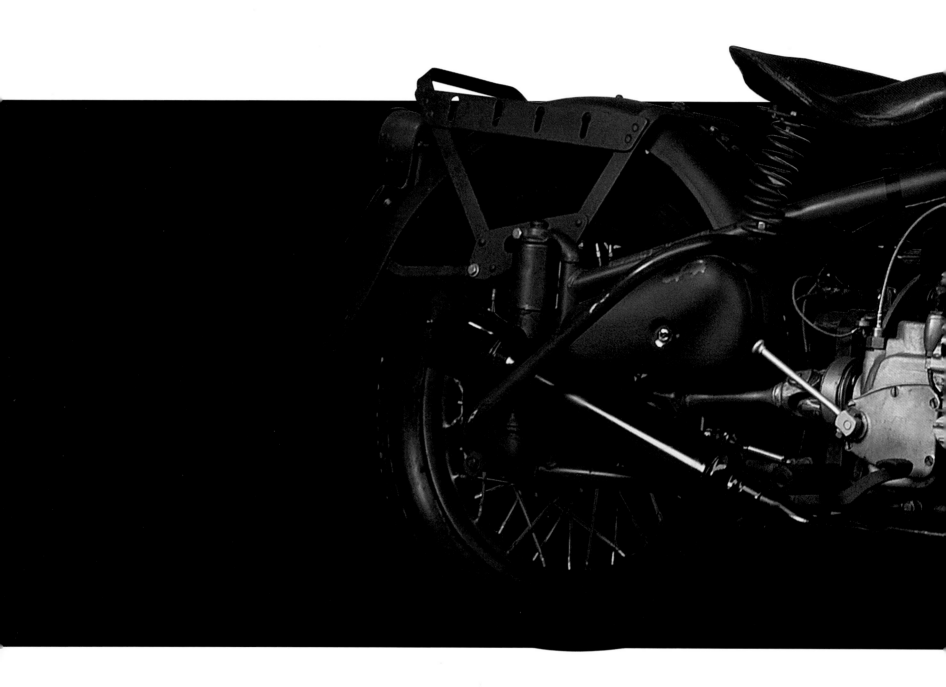

PANHEAD

Panhead E and F (1948)
Panhead Hydra-Glide E (1949–1952) and F (1949–1957)
Panhead F and FL Duo-Glide (1958–1964)
Electra Glide (1965)

After World War II, and once the military surplus had been absorbed by the civilian market, Harley-Davidson resumed normal production with a very diverse list of models: the 45 cubic inch (740 cc) and 74 cubic inch (1200 cc) Flathead, the 61 cubic inch (1000 cc) and 74 cubic inch (1200 cc) OHV Knucklehead, the Servi-Car and sidecars. By 1946, production increased by 30 percent and the Harley-Davidson Company bought, for $1.5 million, a plant in Wauwatosa, a suburb of Milwaukee. The Capitol Drive factory allowed an increase in production to meet the demands of an eager American public that was fresh off wartime restrictions and boosted by the return of soldiers from European fronts. However, Harley-Davidson did not really have any new motorcycles. From the Knucklehead to the Flathead, these were machines designed before the war, and they had aged.

The firm understood the problem and wasted no time in presenting its new 1948 models to dealers at the Schroeder Hotel in Milwaukee on November 27, 1947. This was the largest gathering of American and Canadian Harley-Davidson dealers ever assembled. From the hotel, a train specially chartered for the dealers brought them to the Capitol Drive factory in Wauwatosa, where they discovered the new 61 cubic inch (1000 cc) Panhead, medium compression E Sport Solo, high compression EL Special Sport Solo, medium compression 74 cubic inch (1200 cc) ES Sidecar, medium compression F Sport Solo, high compression FL Special Sport Solo and medium compression FS Sidecar, which replaced the Knucklehead engines in 1948.

These 61 cubic inch (1000 cc) and 74 cubic inch (1200 cc) models were more akin to a modernized Knucklehead than a real new model, though they did bring enormous technological innovations, as the top engine was entirely new. Cylinder heads were now aluminum, seats and valve guides were improved and the top engine tumblers, which operated the valves, were now hydraulic in order to reduce maintenance. The lubrication system used internal ducts that eliminated the Knucklehead's external hoses and reduced leakage. A new oil pump, meanwhile, increased top engine lubrication by 25 percent. The cylinder head covers, which abandoned the bone shape in favor of a pan shape (hence the nickname "Panhead") now covered them completely and enclosed the rockers and valves. The new double cradle frame was called

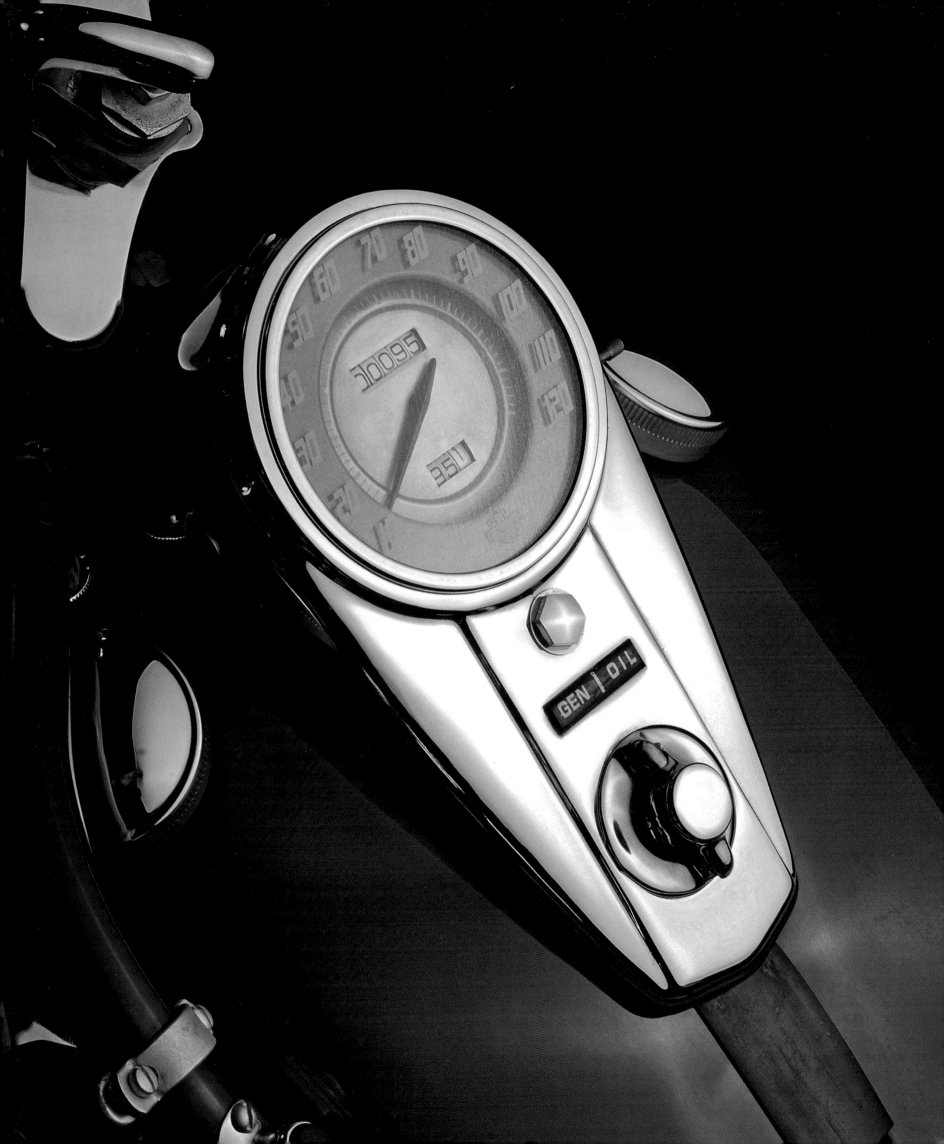

"wishbone" because of the shape of the front tubes. While the Knucklehead's tubes were straight, the curved shape of the Panhead tubes evoked the breastbone of a chicken used to make a wish. The first year of production saw 12,924 Harley-Davidson Panhead motors leave the assembly lines, while only 2377 74 cubic inch (1200 cc) U Flatheads were produced in their last year of production.

Released quickly in 1948, the Panhead motorcycle engine did not yet have a modern element that its English competitors had: a telescopic hydraulic fork, something all of the 61 cubic inch (1000 cc) and 74 cubic inch (1200 cc) lines, now only consisting of models with Panhead E and F engines, adopted as a standard feature in 1949 for the Hydra-Glide.

The Springer fork, meanwhile, remained available as an option. Everything, in fact, on the front of the Hydra-Glide was new: the large headlight, a larger brake drum which offered 34 percent more braking surface, a mudguard molded out of one piece instead of several welded parts and new handlebars and risers adapted to the new fork, whose design would stand as the classic Harley-Davidson look for decades.

102 *The motorcycles with Panhead engines were available in "Hydra-Glide" versions in 1949, receiving the new telescopic fork. An advertising poster for the 1949 FL Hydra Glide equipped with its new fork.*

103 *While the 74 cubic inch (1200 cc) F and FL Panhead replaced their Springer fork with a hydraulic fork in 1949, becoming, in the process, the "Hydra-Glide," the Springer-type fork was still available as an option.*

104 AND 105 THE 74 CUBIC INCH (1200 CC) FLATHEAD
HARLEY-DAVIDSONS WERE NO LONGER IN THE 1949 CATALOG,
AND THE 61 CUBIC INCH (1000 CC) PANHEAD E (LIKE THIS
MODEL, A 74 CUBIC INCH F SERIES) ENTERED THE MODERN ERA
WITH ITS NEW HYDRAULIC FORK, FINISHING AND EQUIPMENT,
PREFIGURING THE DESIGN OF HARLEYS TO THE PRESENT DAY.

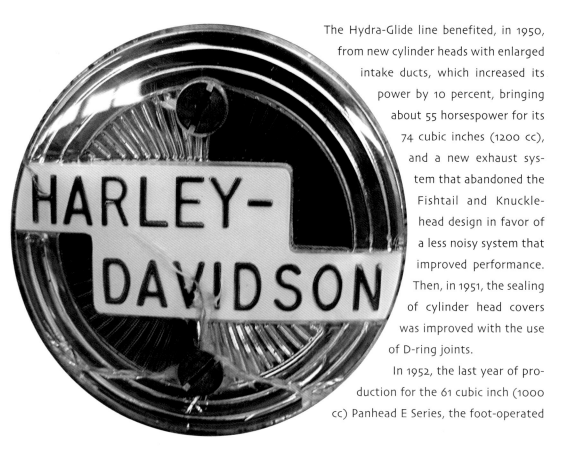

The Hydra-Glide line benefited, in 1950, from new cylinder heads with enlarged intake ducts, which increased its power by 10 percent, bringing about 55 horsepower for its 74 cubic inches (1200 cc), and a new exhaust system that abandoned the Fishtail and Knucklehead design in favor of a less noisy system that improved performance. Then, in 1951, the sealing of cylinder head covers was improved with the use of D-ring joints.

In 1952, the last year of production for the 61 cubic inch (1000 cc) Panhead E Series, the foot-operated transmission was available as an option. The handlebar clutch was assisted by a clutch booster attached to the left tube of the frame that aimed to facilitate the circulation of the clutch cable. This spring mechanism was housed under a long cover resembling a mousetrap, hence the name "Mousetrap."

Models with foot-operated transmissions added an "F" at the end of their name – 61 cubic inch (1000 cc) ELF and 74 cubic inch (1200 cc) FLF – and the slightly modified framework adopted new engine anchors.

The Hydra-Glide, only produced in the 74 cubic inch (1200 cc) F series starting in 1953, saw its hydraulic lifters migrate from the pushrods down to the engine. Closer to the oil pump, they benefitted from a flood of regular oil pressure, which removed the frequent draining problem.

106 AND 107 *STARTING IN 1953, THE HYDRA GLIDES, LIKE THIS*
MODEL, WERE UNIQUELY POWERED BY 74 CUBIC INCH (1200 CC)
ENGINES THAT RECEIVED FEW MECHANICAL CHANGES. CASINGS,
HOWEVER, WERE REDESIGNED TO ALLOW CIRCUITS WITH
DIFFERENT LUBRICATION.

Harley-Davidson celebrated its 50-year anniversary in 1954, even though the birth of the company dated back to 1903. Other significant anniversaries in the future would use the start date of 1903. The Hydra-Glide was given a round medallion decorated with a golden bar and shield and a large "V" overflowing from the front fender. A big horn trumpet, called "horn jubilee," also decorated the Hydra-Glide, which was offered in a variety of solid colors in 1954 but also in a two-tone color at no extra cost. It was also the year of the first fiberglass seats, available as an option. The frame was first modified to accept the jubilee horn, then changed back to the classic wishbone model before being replaced at the end of 1954 by a new straight tube framework, similar to those of the old Knucklehead.

When it came to the mechanics, the internal changes were minimal but the distribution housing cover, which had been eight horizontal stripes, was changed to four.

In 1955, high-compression models took the name FLH (FLHF with footswitch) and enjoyed polished and profiled intake pipes for improved gas inlet, which provided nearly 10 percent more horsepower. The engine again received a few internal modifications, but it was in 1956 that the FLH models saw great improvements, adopting a new Victory camshaft. Providing a superior opening for the valves, it generated 12 percent more power than the standard FL models. This camshaft would be used until 1969 on the FLH models. The cylinder heads were new and now had nine fins on the side of the lifters instead of the previous six.

If the FL and FLH models received very little improvements in 1957, it was because the new Sportster monopolized attention and because it was the last year of the Hydra-Glide.

108 and 109 The 1954 Hydra-Glide had three successive frames. This model from the beginning of the year came with a wishbone-type frame, while the Hydra-Glide marketed at the end of the 1954 was equipped with a frame that featured straight front cradle tubes.

110 AND 111 IN 1957, THE HYDRA-GLIDE WAS COUPLED WITH
SIDECARS AND THE CHASSIS RECEIVED AN "M BOX"
MANUFACTURED BY HARLEY-DAVIDSON WHICH, LIKE THIS MODEL,
WERE FLH AND FL BIKES WITH A HAND-OPERATED CLUTCH AND
WERE PREFERRED OVER MODELS WITH FOOT-OPERATED SYSTEMS.

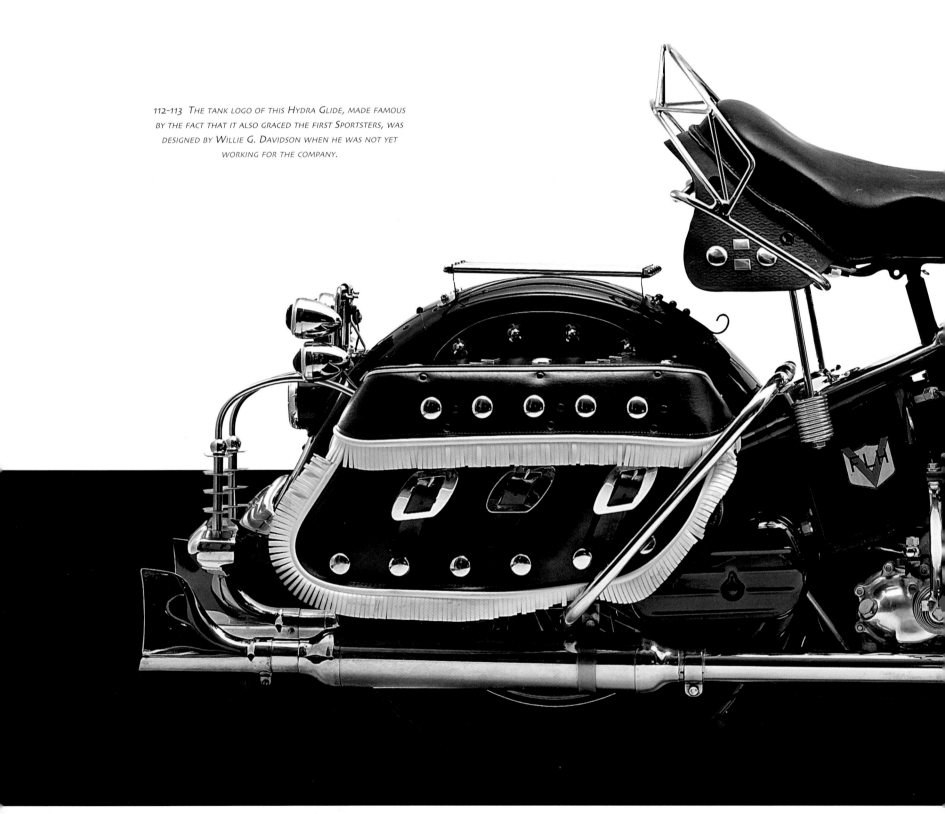

112-113 *The tank logo of this Hydra Glide, made famous by the fact that it also graced the first Sportsters, was designed by Willie G. Davidson when he was not yet working for the company.*

1958–1964: PANHEAD F AND FL DUO-GLIDE, AND ELECTRA-GLIDE

The year 1958 is an historic one for Harley-Davidson, since it is the year of the Duo-Glide's birth. The Hydra-Glide disappeared in favor of the Duo-Glide, which retained the same 74 cubic inch (1200 cc) Panhead engine, but henceforth was housed in a new frame with a swingarm and two rear shock absorbers, in addition to a new hydraulic fork. Harley-Davidson outfitted this new bike with a rear hydraulic brake and the cylinder heads received newly designed fins to improve cooling.

It was available in FL and FLH models with a hand-operated transmission and FLF and FLHF

models with a foot-operated transmission. The "H" models described bikes with high compression. The only complaints about its handling stemmed from police officers in the California Highway Patrol who felt some instability at high speeds above the legal limit. This was a problem Harley-Davidson solved quickly by decreasing the clamping force applied to the steering column. While the Hydra-Glide already had many accessories, Harley-Davidson developed another line for the Duo-Glide, the touring motorcycle par excellence of the era. The company offered an optional windshield, additional headlights,

turn signals, a stylized one-seat or two-seater (the "buddy-seat") with sliding suspension in a tube frame, firewalls, leg guards, a luggage rack and fenders, not to mention its two-tone paint and tank emblems.

Harley-Davidson, which sought to counter the small Japanese motorcycles, would soon start investing in the development of lighter motorcycles, but as the Duo-Glide was quite successful it remained virtually unchanged in subsequent years.

In 1960, it received a new nacelle with a headlight, a more powerful rear brake and minor mechanical modifications. It was not until 1961 that

115 THE DUO GLIDE WAS THE NATURAL EVOLUTION OF THE HYDRA-GLIDE IN 1958. IT RECEIVED A PAIR OF REAR SHOCK ABSORBERS AND FRONT AND REAR SUSPENSION. THE BIG HARLEY-DAVIDSONS CAUGHT UP TO THE STANDARDS OF COMFORT AT THE TIME AND QUICKLY BECAME, LIKE THIS 1961 FLH, THE REFERENCE FOR LUXURY TOURING.

114 THE DUAL EXHAUST OF THIS 1961 DUO GLIDE, WHICH RETAINED INTERCONNECTED TUBES, WAS AN OPTION IN THE ORIGINAL HARLEY-DAVIDSON CATALOG, WHICH APPEARED IN THE MIDDLE OF THE YEAR FOR THIS MODEL.

the Duo-Glide inaugurated the single-fire ignition; each cylinder now had a coil and a separate ignition. This was the last major innovation concerning the Duo-Glide until 1964, when it disappeared from the Harley-Davidson catalog. But for its final year of existence, the Panhead engine would nevertheless still adopt some revolutionary equipment.

Indeed, while the Duo-Glide disappeared with the appearance of the 1965 Panhead engine line, it remained present under the FLB and FL-HB designations with a hand-operated transmission and FLFB and FLHFB models with foot-operated transmissions (the "B" denoted the electric starter). In 1965, the Electra-Glide 74 cubic inch (1200 cc) Panhead motor replaced the Duo-Glide. The Electra-Glide, which was a simple evolution of the Duo-Glide, had a 12-volt electrical system, replacing the old 6-volt system, a modified framework to accept the starter and larger battery, which also involved a new oil tank and internal changes relating to the change in voltage. But basically the bike remained the same, with only the foot-operated transmission models managing to differentiate themselves with their large 5 gallon (19 L) tanks; hand-operated transmission models retained the old 3 gallon (12 L) tanks. This electric starter was first a source of failure as it could not stand high humidity, a problem Harley-Davidson solved by collaborating with the Homelite Corporation. In addition, the larger battery, electric starter and modified framework significantly increased the weight of the bike. To cope with this extra weight, it would be necessary to increase the engine power and efficiency of the braking system and therefore strengthen the chassis to support these changes. In fact, an entirely new bike had to see the light of day to match these requirements.

THE MODEL K

1952–1956: THE MODEL K

After World War II, Harley-Davidson was facing stiff competition from British motorcycle brands such as Triumph and Norton, especially after 1947. These sportbikes seduced Americans and brought forth numerous technical innovations, including foot-operated transmissions. In addition, tax incentives for countries affected by the war did not favor Harley-Davidson. The company responded with the Model K, dubbed the "K Sport," a bike meant to boost sales and regain market share from the Brits.

Thanks to the Marshall Plan, which promoted the import of products manufactured in war-ravaged European countries, English motorcycles with small and medium displacements successfully flooded the U.S. market. Even worse, these UK brands even managed to beat Harley-Davidson on the competitive racing circuit. Beautiful and modern with their foot-operated transmissions and hand-operated clutches, they were lightweight and easy to ride. The first imported bikes were 21 cubic inch (340 cc) Ariels, Royal Enfields, Triumphs and BSAs, though they were soon followed by 30.5 cubic inch (500 cc) Nortons, Ariels and Triumphs. At the end of 1946, almost 10,000 small foreign motorcycles had been sold in the U.S., even though Harley-Davidson had prohibited its dealers from selling them or performing maintenance on them.

The Model K, which was powered by a new 45 cubic inch (740 cc) engine, replaced the WL Flathead block in 1952 and shined on the road and in competition. The K Sport 45 was innovative in relation to other Harley-Davidsons, with its engine and transmission forming a single block and its foot-operated and right channel transmission and clutch attached to the left handlebar. However, its aluminum alloy cylinder heads still retained the side-valves of the Flathead engine. Its chassis was also new thanks to a double cradle frame with a hydraulic fork and a swingarm with two rear shocks. The K was promising on paper, but it still did not perform as well as its English competitors, with a 30 horsepower engine that was sorely lacking in power.

With continued competition from foreign manufacturers, sales of Harley-Davidsons in 1953 fell 20 percent, while the only other major American motorcycle manufacturer, Indian, closed its doors. But the Harley-Davidson Company was determined to persevere. Even though the K models were criticized for their lack of power, their quality frame and the WL side valves, bore and stroke they had inherited meant they could be made much more reliable and efficient with only a few improvements. The bike quickly evolved, and numerous sport versions appeared.

In 1954, Harley-Davidson replaced the 45 cubic inch (740 cc) Model K series with the 55 cubic inch (900 cc) KH Solo Sport, which was still powered by a side valve Flathead engine but now had 38 horsepower, 8 more than the original K. This was an attempt to remain competitive with the English. The new bike's compression ratio was increased from 6:1 to 6.8:1, with a 100 mph (160 km/h) top speed advertised by the manufacturer. On the competitive circuit, a 55 cubic inch (900 cc) KHRM model joined the 45 cubic inch (740 cc) KR and KRTT, which had existed since 1952. The KHK Super Sport Solo was integrated into the commercial market in 1956, as Harley-Davidson was still trying to boost sales of the Model K series with the KHK Cam sport.

In May 1956, the cover of *Enthusiast magazine* featured the newest rock star, Elvis Presley, sitting on a 55 cubic inch (900 cc) KH. That bike, which had appeared in various sport versions tailored to different types of competitions, would soon be customizable, with owners capable of adding racing-related parts to their road bikes. These options made KHs a little more competitive with the English, and the practice would develop in the future as the bike would continue to compete on the professional circuit for years to come.

In 1957, a new bike replaced the Model K series in the Harley-Davidson line, but special competitive designs, like the 45 cubic inch (740 cc) KR and KRTT and the KHRTT were still available. The following year, only the 45 cubic inch (740 cc) KR and KRTT racing models remained in the catalog and they would allow the Milwaukee brand to earn victories on the competitive circuit for many years, long after the end of their commercial availability.

116-117 In 1952, the 45 cubic inch (740 cc) Flathead K Sport model appeared, with the engine and transmission forming a single block. It also had both a foot and a hand-operated clutch, shock absorbers and a fork containing springs and oil. These innovations propelled Haley-Davidson into the modern era.

119 In 1954, THE K MODEL INCREASED ITS CAPACITY FROM
45 CUBIC INCHES (740 CC) TO 55 CUBIC INCHES (900 CC)
AND BECAME THE 55 CUBIC INCH KH SPORT SOLO SPORT.

SERVI-CAR

1932–1973: 45 CI SERVI-CAR G

The big news in 1932 for the 45 cubic inch (740 cc) Harley-Davidsons was their modernization with the evolution of the Model D, which became the Model R. However, 1932 also marked the emergence of a new type of Harley-Davidson vehicle, the Servi-Car, powered by the new 45 cubic inch (740 cc) Flathead engine.

Presented to dealers in the pages of the company newsletter on November 9, 1931, this three-wheeled vehicle was aimed at garages and service stations to facilitate managing and delivering their clients' cars. For example, using a tow bar, the Servi-Car could be towed behind a car and the driver could return to the garage with the Servi-Car. Thanks to its trunk space, the Servi-Car was also used to rapidly transport a mechanic to perform repairs of vehicles on site or for fixing punctured tires.

In the 1932 Harley-Davidson catalog, four different three-speed models were available, all priced at $450. The G came with a small trunk and a tow bar. The GA had a small trunk but no tow bar. The GD had a large trunk but no tow bar, and the GE came with a large trunk and an air tank.

This hybrid vehicle would remain in production for 41 years and, from its front all the way to the seat, its inspiration was the 45 cubic inch (740 cc) Model R 45. The rear, however, consist-

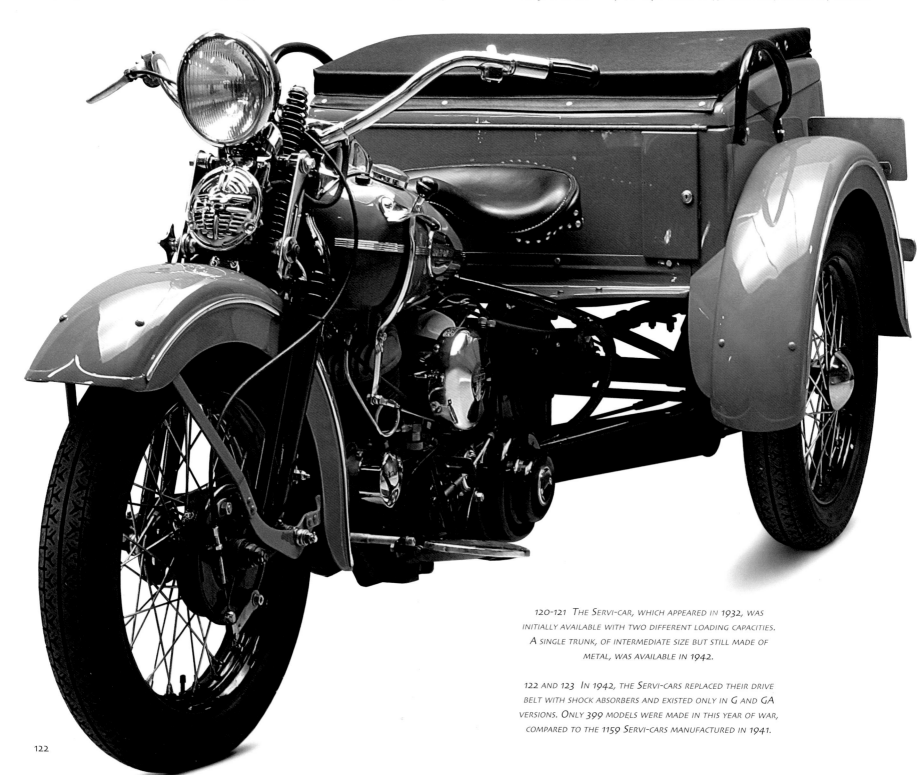

120-121 THE SERVI-CAR, WHICH APPEARED IN 1932, WAS INITIALLY AVAILABLE WITH TWO DIFFERENT LOADING CAPACITIES. A SINGLE TRUNK, OF INTERMEDIATE SIZE BUT STILL MADE OF METAL, WAS AVAILABLE IN 1942.

122 AND 123 IN 1942, THE SERVI-CARS REPLACED THEIR DRIVE BELT WITH SHOCK ABSORBERS AND EXISTED ONLY IN G AND GA VERSIONS. ONLY 399 MODELS WERE MADE IN THIS YEAR OF WAR, COMPARED TO THE 1159 SERVI-CARS MANUFACTURED IN 1941.

ed of an enlarged chassis with a primary drive chain and a secondary drive chain transmission that activated the rear axle differential of the two rear wheels. The rear brake, a drum attached to the axle, was an identical model to that fitted on the 74 cubic inch (1200 cc) Flathead Harley-Davidson. To help inexperienced drivers, the wheelbase of the rear wheels was identical to that of automobiles, thereby allowing them to drive in the deep tracks left by cars in mud or snow. The steel frame behind the driver was connected to the bike portion by blades and a shaft and by coil springs at the rear.

Since 1933, three-speed models of the R 45 Solo, which used the Servi-Car in 1932, were replaced by a three-speed constant mesh transmission with reverse gear, and the TDM model, with a large trunk and tow bar, was added to the line.

The 45 cubic inch (740 cc) Flathead engine would experience a very long career thanks to the Servi-Car, which it equipped until 1973. From 1932 to 1936 it was the R 45 engine, which was replaced by that of the W 45 series. This came with a new lubrication system in 1937. That same year, each of the Servi-Car's rear wheels were equipped with a drum brake, and like other Harley-Davidson models it benefited from a new modern design and look.

Originally intended for transportation and service professionals, the Servi-Car quickly attracted an administrative clientele, including postal workers and especially the police, who used it mainly in the city to monitor traffic and parking. These represented the main users of the Servi-Car at the end of its career, as some U.S. police departments were still using Servi-Cars in the 1990s. Shortly after its appearance, many private advertising companies were attracted by the Servi-Car, as the vehicle was an excellent advertising medium. Indeed, the rear deck and large trunk of the Servi-Car was perfect for use as an advertising medium or simply to brandish a company's logo.

The model GE, which was available on order in 1938 and 1939, disappeared from the line in 1940. In 1941, the Servi-Car models, like other Harley-Davidson bikes, adopted 16-inch (40 cm) wheels. In 1942, a single trunk, of intermediate size but still made of metal, replaced the two previous models so that the line now consisted of the G (with tow bar) and GA (without tow bar).

The 1951 Servi-Car adopted a hydraulic braking system. Then, in 1958, it abandoned the Springer fork in favor of a telescopic hydraulic fork like that of the Harley-Davidson Hydra-Glide.

While it was no longer being used to tow and deliver automobiles, in 1964 there was only one GE model that did not come with tow bar. It did, however, come with an electric starter. It was, in fact, the first Harley-Davidson series to be equipped with an electric starter. In 1967, the metal trunk gave way to a fiberglass model, and at the end of 1973 the Servi-Car's rear wheel was equipped with disc brakes instead of drums. However, these were the last models produced, as they were not in the 1974 Harley-Davidson catalog.

125 *AMONG THE VARIOUS AGENCIES THAT USED SERVI-CARS, POLICE FORCES AROUND THE COUNTRY STUCK WITH HARLEY-DAVIDSON SERVI-CARS THROUGHOUT THE ENTIRE EXISTENCE OF THE VEHICLE. THIS 1969 GE MODEL WAS EQUIPPED WITH A FIBERGLASS TRUNK, WHICH REPLACED THE METAL TRUNKS IN 1967.*

SMALL ENGINES

USA Productions: S 125 (1947–1952), ST 165 (1953–1959)

125 B Hummer (1955–1959), 165 BT (1960–1962)

175 BT (1962–1966)

Scooter: Topper 165 (1960–1965)

Italian Productions: Sprint 250 and 350 (1961–1974)

M-50, M-65 and Shortster (1965–1968), Rapido (1968–1977)

Baja and SR 100 (1970–1974), SS/SX 175 and 250 (1974–1978)

USA PRODUCTIONS: S 125 (1947–1952), ST 165 (1953–1959), 125 B HUMMER (1955–1959), 165 BT (1960–1962), 175 BT (1962–1966)

At the end of World War II, Harley-Davidson had to rejuvenate its civilian motorcycles, which had not really changed since the conflict began. Moreover, these bikes did not meet the expectations of a new, young and eager clientele who were calling for light and cheap bikes. Fortunately, as compensation for its war effort, Harley-Davidson and BSA received the rights to produce the 125 DKW RT, a German two-stroke, in 1947.

Since the end of the war, British bikes with small engines had successfully won the hearts of younger Americans. In this still unexplored new market, the Excelsior, the Francis-Barnett (with a Villiers engine), the 125 Royal Enfield and the James all found success on U.S. soil. Harley-Davidson dealers were calling for motorcycles with small and medium displacements to retain customers who were increasingly seduced by these light, modern and efficient motorcycles. One of these wishes would soon be granted.

At the Harley-Davidson congress in November 1947, the dealers discovered, in addition to the previously announced Panhead, the new S 7.5 cubic inch (125 cc) Harley-Davidson, a two-stroke single-cylinder engine with a three-speed transmission that provided about 3 horsepower and had a small "peanut" tank. This bike was aimed directly at young people.

It joined the 1948 line and met the expectations of the new young and dynamic customers who were looking for luxury and comfort but were too inexperienced for large, heavy V-Twins. The newest Harley-Davidson performed better than its English rivals, and at $325 each they sold out in six months, with 10,117 produced for the first year. While machines with Villiers engines had a top speed of 40 mph (65 km/h), the S 125 Harley-Davidson reached 49 mph (80 km/h) and was

126-127 The smaller two-stroke motorcycles from 1948 were built from plans for the German 125 DWK, which Harley-Davidson received as compensation for its war effort. In 1951, their Girder fork was replaced with a Tele-Glide Fork, as on this model.

128-129 The 175 Bobcat from 1966 had a fiberglass shell that covered the tank, supporrted the saddle and served as a rear fender. It was the last small-displacement Harley-Davidson model from the Hummer line.

much more reliable. With a rigid frame and a Girder (parallelogram) fork, it changed little over the following years. However, its fork was replaced with a telescopic Tele-Glide fork and enveloping fenders in 1951.

Equipped with foldable footrests in 1952, it gained a few cubic inches in 1953 and was available in a 10 cubic inch (165 cc) ST, producing about 5.5 horses, and a 10 cubic inch (165 cc) STU model. The power of the latter was restricted so that it had less than 5 horsepower, allowing people to drive without having to get a license. This displacement corresponded to 10 cubic inches (165 cc), which earned the bike the nickname "Super 10." This would be the reference point for the 1954 model.

In March 1955, a new bike appeared with a small two-stroke single-cylinder engine, the 7.5 cubic inch (125 cc) B Hummer, which in fact represented the return of the S 125 since both bikes had the same bore and stroke. The 10 cubic inch (165 cc) ST and STU and the 125 B Hummer replaced their 19-inch (50 cm) wheels with 18-inch (45 cm) wheels in 1956. While the first 7.5 cubic inch (125 cc) S was equipped with a front brake, the 125 B Hummer model, introduced in 1955, did not have one. But it did get a front brake in 1957 and these little bikes received only minor changes until their final year of existence in 1959.

The new 1960 models, the two-stroke BT Super 10 and BTU Super 10 models, were actually ST models redone to suit the trends of the time. They received 16-inch (40 cm) wheels in 1961 and, in 1962, Harley-Davidson expanded its offering of small engines. This consisted of the 10.5 cubic inch (175 cc) BT Pacer (a BT Super 10 with increased engine capacity), the 10 cubic inch (165 cc) BTU Pacer (formerly a BTU Super 10), the 10 cubic inch (165 cc) BTF Ranger Off-Road Trail (formerly a BT, but without lights, front fenders, shortened rear fenders, 18-inch (45 cm) wheels and Buckhorn handlebars), and the 10.5 cubic inch (175 cc) BTH Scat On/Off Road (a road and all-terrain version of the BT Pacer).

In 1963, only these bikes remained: the BT Pacer Street, BTH Scat Trail and BTU Pacer (a version that still had less than 5 horsepower, despite the displacement). All of these models abandoned the rigid frame in favor of a frame with a swingarm and a rear suspension placed under the engine, like the current Softails. These models went unchanged in 1964, but the BTU Pacer model was no longer in the 1965 line.

In 1966, Harley-Davidson only produced the 10.5 cubic inch (175 cc) BTH Bobcat, which was a modernized version of the BT Pacer with a fiberglass mono-hull from the rear fender to the tank, for supporting the seat and covering the gas tank, and a fiberglass front fender. But this was the last year of production for the American small engines, as Harley-Davidson had decided to rely on Aermacchi-manufactured models for this category of bikes.

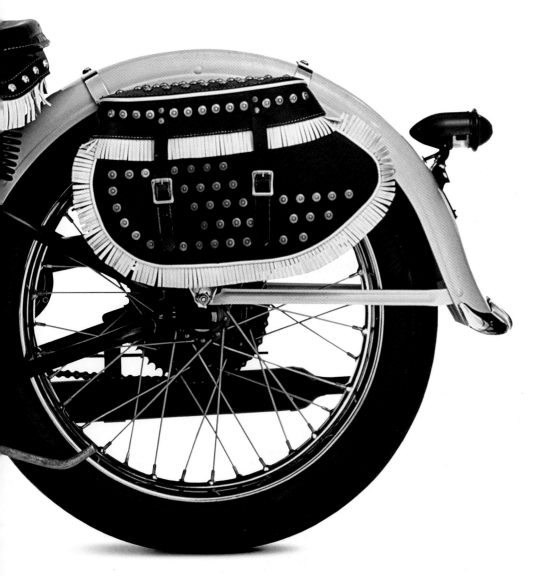

130-131 *THE 1955 MODEL ST 165 HAD ITS CARBURETOR ENCLOSED BEHIND THE ENGINE AND ALSO A REDIMENSIONED KICK.*

SCOOTER: TOPPER 165 (1960–1965)

The 10 cubic inch (160 cc) Topper scooter, which appeared with the 1960 line, was Harley-Davidson's answer to the Italian Vespa and Lambretta scooters that had invaded college campuses. It appeared at the same time as the BT Super models, with whom it shared the same two-stroke block propellant cylinder taken from the first S 125 (the engine capacity was increased in 1953).

In 1960, 3,801 copies of the two Topper models were manufactured and sold for $430 each. They came in two versions: the A, which provided about 6 horsepower, and the AU Topper, which had 5 horsepower despite the power supply being restricted, which allowed unlicensed drivers in some states. The engine was positioned horizontally with a primary automatic belt transmission and a chain at the rear wheel. The fork was balanced with shocks and, in addition to a new rear brake at the right foot, the left handlebar had a front brake lever that could serve as a parking brake by locking a cam. Under the seat was a trunk used to transport oil that could be mixed with gasoline at service stations, but this space was generally used to carry school books and other small hardware.

The high compression AH model, which replaced the Model A in 1961, had 9 horsepower, which allowed the Topper to better compete with its rivals. Both Toppers, the AH and AU, were given sidestands and could be equipped with a sidecar or a "utility box" for transporting goods. This box simply replaced the sidecar on the additional chassis. The price climbed that year to $445 and only 1341 Toppers were produced.

The Topper would continue to undergo minor changes but production would steadily decrease, as initial success thanks to a successful advertising campaign and critical praise could not be sustained. While 800 AH Toppers were manufactured in 1964, only 25 AUs left the assembly line in its last year of production. The 1965 AH Topper was identical to that of the previous year and the 500 copies produced by the Harley-Davidson factory were the last of the series.

132 HARLEY-DAVIDSON, WHICH WANTED TO MEET A GROWING DEMAND FOR THE TYPE OF BIKES COMING MAINLY FROM ITALY, INTRODUCED THE TOPPER SCOOTER AS THE IDEAL VEHICLE FOR DAILY COMMUTES AND FAMILY FUN.

132-133 *The AH Topper model replaced the A model in 1961 by offering increased power and an optional sidecar. The 1962 model with sidecar is pictured.*

In April 1960, Harley-Davidson acquired half of Aeronatica-Macchi and created Aermacchi Harley-Davidson, a European division that would produce small single-cylinder motorcycles. The Harley-Davidson International branch was soon created as the company sought to grow its exports in the face of rising competition on American soil.

At the end of 1961, and following an agreement signed in 1960 with Aermachi, Harley-Davidson added a four-stroke horizontal single-cylinder motorcycle to its line of Sprint 250 C, which would remain in its catalog until 1968. Several sport versions would also be released. This bike was originally a 16-horsepower Ala Verde created in 1959. It would become the Sprint C Wisconsin and would arrive on American soil in 1961. From then on it would retain the Sprint C name.

In 1962 the power of this motorcycle was increased to 18 horsepower and an offroad version was also available, with the high compression Sprint H model producing 21 horsepower. The four-speed bikes used cast-iron cylinders and aluminum cylinder heads.

For the Sprint H, the 5-gallon (18 L) tank was reduced to 3 gallons (13 L), the wheels went from 17 inches (43 cm) to 18 inches (46 cm), the exhaust was raised, the fork equipped with rubber bellows and, thanks to a new carburetor and exhaust and an increased compression ratio, the power rose to 25 horsepower. For the competition circuit, the light and exhaust-free R models could compete with foreign bikes in regional events, and they were soon joined by two-stroke bikes like the CR-flat track, CRS motocross and the Clubman Racer Sprint SS.

In 1966, the displacement of the 15 cubic inch (250 cc) engine remained the same, but the bore and stroke were modified with an increased bore and a shorter stroke. The bikes would not experience any more major changes until 1969.

AMF took over Harley-Davidson in 1969 and

replaced the 15 cubic inch (250 cc) Sprint with the 21 cubic inch (350 cc) Sprint SS, a road motorcycle called the Street Scrambler. In 1970, the 27-horsepower 350 SS Sprint had a dry clutch, but it kept a four-speed transmission and adopted two large exhaust mufflers on each side of the bike. In 1971 the Sprint SX-350, a trail/enduro type model, joined the SS-350.

Harley-Davidson still offered the 350 SS and SX with a simple frame, a four-speed transmission and a kick start in 1972, but in 1973 and 1974

these bikes had a five-speed transmission, a double cradle frame and an electric starter. Nevertheless, it was the final year for these four-stroke single-cylinder engines. During the career of the 21 cubic inch (350 cc) engine, these bikes were also available in special competitive models: ERS, CRS and CRTT.

AMF-Harley-Davidson replaced its 21 cubic inch (350 cc) SS and SX four-stroke engines with the 15 cubic inch (250 cc) SS and SX two-stroke, five-speed engines in 1974. These models re-

134-135 *The Leggero M-65 and M-65 Sport, produced until 1972, evolved from the M-50 and M-50 Sport, which were imported in 1966.*

mained in the catalog until 1977. The SST 250 of 1976 and 1977 was just an SS 250 whose front drum brake was replaced with a disc brake, and the MX 250 in 1977 and 1978 was the cross racing version that came with a two-stroke single-cylinder 15 cubic inch (250 cc) engine. But 1978 was the last year of collaboration with Aermachi in Italy, which meant an end to Harley-Davidson models with small and medium-sized two-stroke engines and led to the birth of the Cagiva.

SS and SX models with two-stroke engines were an attempt to counter the Yamaha DT1, whose all-terrain models had entered the market in 1968 and would monopolize it in the 1970s.

The same policy applied to smaller displace-ment bikes. The 8 cubic inch (125 cc) Rapido MLS model, which had a single-cylinder two-stroke engine and four-speed transmission, appeared in 1968. It was replaced by the five-speed TX in 1973, which would become the SX in 1974 and 1975. The SXT, released between 1975 and 1977, was an SX with a similar look to that of more powerful engines like the 11 cubic inch (175 cc) SX in 1974 and 1975 and the 15 cubic inch (250 cc) SX.

However, because this complicated series changed so often and because dealers were limited in their ability to meet the expectations of young and amateur off-roaders, to say nothing of the competitive prices of Japanese motorcy-cles, Harley-Davidson could not break the Japanese dominance in the trail category. Road bikes equipped with the same engines and transmissions fared little better, including the 8 cubic inch (125 cc) Rapido ML from 1968 to 1972 and the 8 cubic inch (125 cc) SS and 11 cubic inch (175 cc) SS from 1975 to 1977.

During this period in the 1960s and 1970s, Harley-Davidson tried to diversify and attract a younger clientele. In 1965, the first 3 cubic inch (50 cc) moped appeared, with a single-cylinder two-stroke three-speed engine that Harley-Davidson had manufactured in Italy by Aermachi. It would be called the M-50. The more attractive M-50 Sport, made on the same basic

136-137 IN EUROPE, AERMACCHI HARLEY-DAVIDSON PRODUCED MOTORCYCLES WITH SMALLER ENGINE CAPACITIES, INCLUDING THE 250 SPRINT, WHICH, LIKE THIS 1966 SPRINT H, HAD A HORIZONTAL FOUR-STROKE STARTING IN 1961.

mechanics, would accompany it in 1966. Poor in performance compared to Japanese models, they would give way to the M-65 and M-65 Sport in 1967. Stronger and more aesthetically appealing, these models were not as successful as expected. They would become the Leggero M-65 and M-65 Sport in 1970 and would disappear by the end of 1972.

The Baja SR 100, which appeared in 1970, had a five-speed two-stroke 6 cubic inch (98 cc) engine and was the all-terrain version of the Leggero. The Baja was also available in the MSR-100, a competitive racing model.

Built in 1971 but sold with the 1972 line, the single cylinder Shortster MC-65, with a two-stroke engine and three-speed transmission, was

a "mini-bike." It was replaced by the 5 cubic inch (90 cc) X-90, which had a four-speed transmission, and the Z-90, a small dirt bike with the same engine, from 1973 to 1975.

During the 1970s, the company's diversification continued with golf carts and snowmobiles, but like the small and mid-sized bikes, they were not as successful as expected.

IRON SPORTSTER

XL Sportster 55 (1957–1959)
XLH and XLCH 55 Sportster (1958–1971)
XR 750 (1970–1980)
XLH (1972–1985), XLCH (1972–1979)
XLS (1979–1985) and XLX (1983–1985)
XLT Touring and Café Racer XLCR (1977–1979)
XR 1000 (1983–1984)

THE XL SPORTSTER 55 (1957–1959), XLH AND XLCH 55 SPORTSTER (1958–1971)

THE SPORTSTER XL 55

A new motorcycle concept replaced the KH models in 1957 and was designed to respond to the demands of a younger demographic. This new machine would finally compete with the popular English bikes, since the Sportster XL 55 cubic inch (900 cc) with overhead valves was for all intents and purposes a modern bike. Indeed, the cylinder heads of this bike, which had its origins in the 1952 K 45 model, and which ended up taking on the Flathead engine used on the 1929 D 45, were not made out of aluminum but iron.

The engine of the 1957 Sportster took the low motor of the KH with a modified bore and stroke, which allowed higher speeds while maintaining a similar 53.9 cubic inch (880 cc) displacement. This would be listed as 55 cubic inch (900 cc) in the catalog, hence the XL 55 name for the Sportster. It retained a valve camshaft, but it was larger and now overhead instead of lateral. Despite modern aluminum parts, such as pistons, and a 7.5:1 compression ratio, it generated only 40 hp at 5500 rpm, which was less than the English bikes on the market. Another drawback was that this new Sportster retained the same design as the 1952 Model K, with only one seat, a large tank, a huge rollover fork supporting a massive headlight and large buckhorn handlebars. Not surprisingly, enthusiasts of high performance sports motorcycles were not really impressed. Harley-Davidson produced 1,983 civilian model XL Sportsters, plus 418 XLAs destined for the army in 1957.

These sales figures were equivalent to those of the first K models produced in 1952. The Sportster, therefore, did not have an easy time upon its debut, while its price ($1,103) also did not sufficiently differentiate it from the FL 74 Hydra Glide Sport Solo ($1,167).

138-139 The Sportster XR 1000 adopted the design of the Racer XR 750 with its two carburetors mounted on the right side and its exhaust out the left.

140-141 The 1957 XL Sportster was a new model but it retained a heavy design, not unlike that of the K model that it replaced, positioning itself as a young, dynamic and aggressive machine.

141 top The 1957 Prospectus Sportster, a modern motorcycle for dynamic men.

By 1958, Harley-Davidson had corrected its Sportster, with improved performance thanks to a higher compression ratio that increased power. Models were now also specialized and the Sportster was available in four versions: the medium compression XL, the high compression XLH and the XLCH and XLC, which were not street legal and which had a different compression ratio. The XLC conserved the medium compression engine architecture of the XL but with the racing equipment of the XLCH, while the XLH adopted the aesthetics of the XL with the high compression engine of the XLCH. The "H" designated high compression models and the "C" designated competitive models. The high compression H models (9:1 instead of 7.5:1) were equipped with bigger valves, pistons with very curved caps and 45 horsepower. The C competition models came with magneto ignition, a separate exhaust, a reduced and streamlined dressing, a small "peanut" tank, a short rear fender and optional raised pots for a look that outlined future Sportster generations. These competitive models were devoid of headlights and were much lighter and better performing than other Sportsters.

The XLC was manufactured in 1958 and only 42 copies of the XL were produced in 1959, its final year of existence (compared to 579 in 1958). The XLCH was modified to be street legal in 1959, with the XLH becoming the more touring-friendly bike. The XLH, designed for riders who wanted to own a machine that was better equipped for the road than the XLCH, became a dual-use bike with its new equipment, ready for both road and off-road use. It also benefited from accessories that improved its comfort and ease of use, with a battery and coil ignition for easy starting.

The headlight of the 1959 Sportster was attached to the fork via a small cradle, which served as a support to the counter. This would become a recurring element of the Sportster, one that is still present on these bikes in the 21st century, much like the exhaust system, which came with separate silencers arranged one above the other on the right side of the bike. This optional exhaust would soon be modified and become the legendary "Shorty Duals" in 1963.

In 1958, a competitive model, the Sportster XLRTT Tourist Trophy Racer 55, joined the KR Track Racer 45 and the KRTT Tourist Trophy Racer 45. Equipped with a different crankshaft, pistons and special camshafts, bigger valves, lighter rods, rocker arms and KR rods, it generated 60 horsepower. It would be produced until 1966.

In 1960, the XL disappeared and the XLH and XLCH received LF shock absorbers, but only the XLCH replaced its 18-inch (46 cm) front wheel with a 19-inch (48 cm) wheel, while the rear wheel remained 18 inches (46 cm). Some copies were equipped with polyester bags, a windshield and a luggage rack designed for coastal patrols and the army, and a "police" model was developed in 1961. An optional double seat was available in 1961 along with a T-shaped aluminum fork in 1962. The XLH and XLCH received a new transmission, exhaust and a shorter kick, while the XLCH got an improved magneto and an ignition key in 1963. Large drum brakes and aluminum rocker guides were adopted in 1964. Changes continued to be made ever year, but sales remained modest.

In 1965, the XLH and XLCH abandoned their lead adjustable handlebars for the benefit of an automatic feed and were given 12-volt electrical equipment. This first year with the 12-volt system, the Sportster had two 6-volt batteries, as

the XLCH lacked the space to house a 12-volt battery. The XLH received a new tank which reduced its fuel capacity to 3.7 gallons (14 L).

In 1966, the new "P Cams," which were sharper, replaced the Linkert carburetor with a Tillotson diaphragm and provided 15 percent more power. Sales of the XLCH and 900 XLH finally began to progress. The frames of the XLH and XLCH were amended in 1967, but only the XLH kept an electric starter. The two Sportster models received new shock absorbers and a new hydraulic fork in 1968, while the XLH abandoned its kick start and the optional small peanut tank.

In 1969, the Sportster was delivered with a dual exhaust system and a balance pipe between the two separate silencers, and in 1970 the XLCH abandoned magneto ignition in favor of a coil ignition and switches.

The AMF/Harley-Davidson logo first appeared on all models of the range in 1971, and the Sportster replaced its dry clutch with an oil bath clutch. The Sportster XLH was proposed, in 1970 and 1971, with a peculiar option at the rear which was called a "boat tail." Success, however, was not in the cards, and in order to shed inventory some dealers were automatically given Sportsters with this finish. Most often, dealers and customers replaced this rear option with a fender and a traditional light, at their own expense. This particular model, which at the time was called the "Fender Nacel," "Fast Back" and "Boat Tail," was designed by Willie G. Davidson, who had been with the company since 1963. Davidson had wanted to modernize the look of this bike with this polyester element manufactured at the Tomahawk factory, which had been acquired by Harley-Davidson in 1963 and was located about 300 miles (480 km) north of Milwaukee.

143 The Sportster engine retained its initial 55 cubic inch (900 cc) engine from 1957 to 1971. However, it was available in two versions in 1958, including a sporty model, like this 1965 XLCH.

XR 750 (1970–1980)

After the disappearance of its last American competitor in 1953, Harley-Davidson won the annual Grand National Dirt Track Championship with the KR 750, which was powered by Flathead engines. But in 1963, Dick Mann beat Harley-Davidson by winning the title with BSA and Matchless motorcycles. However, Roger Reiman in 1964, and then Bart Markel in 1965 and 1966, restored the title to Harley-Davidson before Gary Nixon won two consecutive championships riding a Triumph in 1967 and 1968. Although Harley-Davidson was able to regain the title in 1969 with Mert Lawwill, the KR was overwhelmed by its competition and the Milwaukee firm commissioned two engineers for a new bike project.

Race director Dick O'Brien and Pieter Zylstra, who designed the new engine, produced the first XR 750, which was built on the foundations of the XL Sportster and the KR. With a shorter stroke and the cylinder bore of the 55 cubic inch (900 cc) Sportster XL retained, the 46 cubic inch (750 cc) XR had the engine capacity required to compete on the competitive racing circuit. Harley-Davidson used aluminum cylinder heads on its Big Twin for decades, but for simple economic reasons the Sportster XLR's cast-iron cylinder heads were chosen. They received larger valves and a camshaft derived from that of the KR. Incorporated into Harley-Davidson in 1970, 200 copies were produced to meet American Motorcycle Association regulations and to be able to compete in dirt-track competitions.

The best riders of the day received the XRs, and they discovered a motorcycle that heated up intensely before cracking and whose single carburetor could not sufficiently supply the combustion chambers. Triumph took home the title in 1970 and BSA won it in 1971. Harley-Davidson was looking for solutions and many different cylinder heads were tested. The initial configuration, similar to the original bikes, had a single carburetor feeding the two heads, which O'Brien changed by placing two carburetors on the right side. Then the carburetor of the front cylinder head was placed on the right side of the rear and the carburetor of the rear cylinder head migrated to the left frontal position. The last version included cylinder heads with admissions on the right side of the rear and an outlet at the front right side for the front cylinder and on the front left for the rear cylinder. Despite these attempts, which produced a satisfactory amount of power, the XR still had problems, as the increase

145 THE FIRST XR 750 WITH A CAST-IRON ENGINE HAD EXHAUST OUTLETS ON THE RIGHT AND WAS POWERED BY A SINGLE CARBURETOR FOR TWO CYLINDERS.

in compression ratio and horsepower still caused it to heat up and crack.

Harley-Davidson needed to invest to develop an XR equipped with aluminum engines. About half of the cast-iron engines produced failed to pass muster and the O'Brien team began working on a new concept. The idea was still to create a 45 degree V-Twin with the two rods on the same crankpin, a tumbled distribution and two valves per cylinder, with an engine similar to the cast-iron XR. But the sides were different, as the fins of the cylinders were now oversized and each had its own Mikuni carburator placed on the right side of the back, while the exhaust exited out the front left of each cylinder. The engine weighed 17.5 pounds (8 kg) less than the cast-iron version and it retained the same chassis. The Harley-Davidson catalog included many parts and accessories for this bike, while the 200 copies produced in order to test the aluminum XR 750 were available in 1972.

While this new XR originally offered 73 horsepower, once tweaked by the Harley-Davidson racing team it generated 83.9 to 7800 rpm and won the title at the Grand National Championship in 1972. However, in the two years following Harley-Davidson could not compete with Kenny Roberts' Yamaha 750, which was derived from the base of the 650 XS. Starting in 1975, the XR 750s dominated the professional circuit until 1983. Following this, only Honda succeeded in stealing the title from Harley-Davidson, in 1984, 1985, 1986, 1987 and 1993. Harley-Davidson has remained unbeaten since then. The last XR completely built by Harley-Davidson was in 1975, but work was still being done to improve performance, and a new generation of engines, provided by Harley-Davidson in 1990, generated 90 horsepower, with an electronic ignition, two spark plugs per cylinder and a compression ratio of 12.5:1. These engines and their derivatives eventually generated 100 horsepower, which seems like a little, but for dirt-track competition pure power is not the only factor to consider. Unlike asphalt, the oval track is best navigated by exploiting the power of the V-Twin engine configuration of the XR. The chassis also must be taken into account with every individual race, as the frame and fork face extreme stress and pressure throughout, given the curves and angles of the track. Following trials, it was noted that the framework required a certain flexibility to provide maximum efficiency, as the more rigid frames tested, using the same engines and drivers on the same track, posted slower race times.

XLH (1972–1985), XLCH (1972–1979), XLS (1979–1985) AND XLX (1983–1985)

In 1972 the two Sportsters, XLH and XLCH, by simply increasing the bore went from 55 cubic inches (900 cc) to 61 cubic inches (1000 cc), delivering 61 hp and a compression ratio of 9:1. A small "peanut" fuel tank and seat accentuated its racy styling, and in 1973 it received a single front disc brake and a Japanese Kayaba fork. The indicators and the accelerator cable with automatic recall by progressive spring carburetors were added in 1974. The law required a foot-operated transmission at the left foot and a brake pedal at the right foot in 1975, and Sportster inverted its controls. In 1976, the

Sportster, like other Harley-Davidson models, was also available in a special anniversary edition celebrating 200 years of United States independence: the "Liberty Edition." The 1977 Sportster range received new casings with a direct outlet on the left of the axis selector and a modified frame that allowed the extraction of the new oil pump without removing the engine. The 1978 Sportster XLH 1000 was available in a limited edition with special painting celebrating the 75th anniversary of Harley-Davidson. The 1978 Sportster was equipped with a dual front disc and a Siamese exhaust system. It benefitted from a new

frame with a swing arm on the square section of the XLCR, an electronic ignition and a new location for the oil tank and battery.

From 1979, the XLS, named the Roadster shortly after its appearance, joined the XLH and XLCH. In essence it was a Sportster XLH with a Low Rider look, an extended fork, a 16-inch (40 cm) rear wheel, Siamese exhaust system, drag bar handlebars, a two-level seat and a sissy bar. It reproduced the basic features of other Sportsters, which that same year had adopted a rear brake disc and an optional kick start.

146 THE XLH SPORTSTER WAS AVAILABLE IN 1970 AND 1971 WITH A UNIQUE FIBERGLASS HULL OPTION. ITS BACK WAS CALLED "BOAT TAIL."

The XLCH disappeared from the catalog in 1980, and a base version of the XLH Sportster, dubbed Hugger, was available with optional shortened shock absorbers and a refined seat. The XLH saw its fork shortened in 1981 to reduce the height of the seat and, like the XLS, it came with several options: spoke or aluminum wheels, 16-inch (40 cm) or 18-inch (45 cm) rear wheels and either a 2.2 (8 L) or 3.3 gallon tank (12.5 L).

In 1982, the two Sportsers were given a lighter and more rigid frame, with a repositioned battery and oil tank as well as a larger rear disc. Their compression ratio was lowered to 8:1 by adopting a thicker head gasket. That year, the Sportster celebrated its 25th anniversary and it was available in specially decorated anniversary models.

In 1983, the XLH and XLS were given a new ignition, the V Fire III, with an advance correction system. The XLH adopted raised handlebars and a 3.3 gallon tank (12.5 L) tank, while the XLS received a center console on a bigger 3.8 gallon (14 L) tank.

Faced with Japanese competition, sales of the Sportster declined for several years, which encouraged Harley-Davidson to design a more competitively priced motorcycle. The XLX 61, a stripped down version of the Sportster painted in black, was sold at the very attractive price of $6,995 to great fanfare. The equipment was minimal, with a small 2.25 gallon (8.5 L) peanut tank, a simple odometer on top of the headlight, a solo seat, black exhaust system with two tubes and aluminum wheels, but also an engine block that performed as efficiently as other Sportsters and which benefited from an advanced electronic system. By itself, this XLX, with 4892 copies produced, surpassed the production of all other Sportsers combined in 1983.

147 IN 1979, THE SPORTSTER XLH AND XLCH LOST THEIR KICK, WHICH BECAME AN OPTION, BUT THEY DID RECEIVE A REAR DISC BRAKE.

XLT TOURING AND XLCR CAFÉ RACER (1977–1979)

The Sportster family was enriched by two models in 1977, the XLT Touring and the XLCR Cafe Racer painted entirely in black, with a new frame, spoked wheels, a dual front disc brake, a single rear disc brake and a Siamese exhaust system. Among the many references used to identify the Sportster range since its inception, the XLCR (more commonly known as "Café Racer") profoundly marked the history of Harley-Davidson, while the XLT Touring was more of a secondary motorcycle.

The XLT was a Sportster XLH adorned with a big, comfortable seat, a large FX Super Glide tank and FLH polyester seats taken from the Electra Glide. Its large handlebars and windshields provided a comfortable touring drive for a motorcycle that did not correspond to the Harley-Davidson customer base at the time. It disappeared from the range in 1979.

The Sportster XLCR Cafe Racer, designed by Willie G. Davidson, Lou Netz and Jim Aubert from the company's racing department, was an American sportsbike that innovated and aimed to revive the brand in the face of competition from Japanese motorcycles. It was presented in Daytona, a place that mixed competition and customization, before hitting the market. The press was enthusiastic, see-

ing the XLCR as the American counterpoint to the Italian and Japanese motorcycles dominiating the market. In conceiving it, Davidson mixed different elements from high performance bikes. Thus, the seat and fenders were inspired by those of the 750 XR, the drag-bar handlebar came from the world of drag racing and the small wind deflector was inspired by European sportsbikes of the time. This was the first Harley-Davidson series to have two front discs, mounted on molded stick rims.

Its Siamese exhaust, where the collector combined the motor outputs before splitting into a muffler on each side of the bike, was totally black, like the rest of the bike. Its Sportster framework was modified, with the back posts lengthened so that the anchors of the shock absorbers and swingarm were pushed back on the frame. While maintaining a fairly vertical rise, the rear wheel axle shock absorbers provided better handling and a sportier drive. Its engine remained that of the Sportster 1000 XL.

Although the press warmly welcomed the Sportster XLCR, customers did not embrace it as enthusiastically. In addition to its unusual design, which was too ahead of its time and very different from the brand's normal aesthetic criteria, it also had several flaws that amateur sportsbike riders

discovered with use. The driving position was uncomfortable, the footrests too far back for a high handlebar, the small wind deflector bounced wind and rain on the driver. But the main criticism was over its high price ($6,995) compared to other Sportsters and most especially the competition, which offered better machines at lower prices. Its main selling point, and a big reason for its high sticker price, was its cast-iron engine, which provided a unique experience but did not seem very sensible to most sportsbike fans.

Unable to attract new drivers or the traditional Harley-Davidson clientele, the Sportster XLCR was a commercial flop. Only 3,133 copies were produced over three years: 1,923 in 1977, 1,201 in 1978 (with an optional dual seat) and just 9 in 1979. Dealers of the era had to offer huge discounts to get rid of this motorcycle, but it was nevertheless this Sportster's frame, which Davidson reviewed and corrected, that would equip all Sportsters from 1979 on.

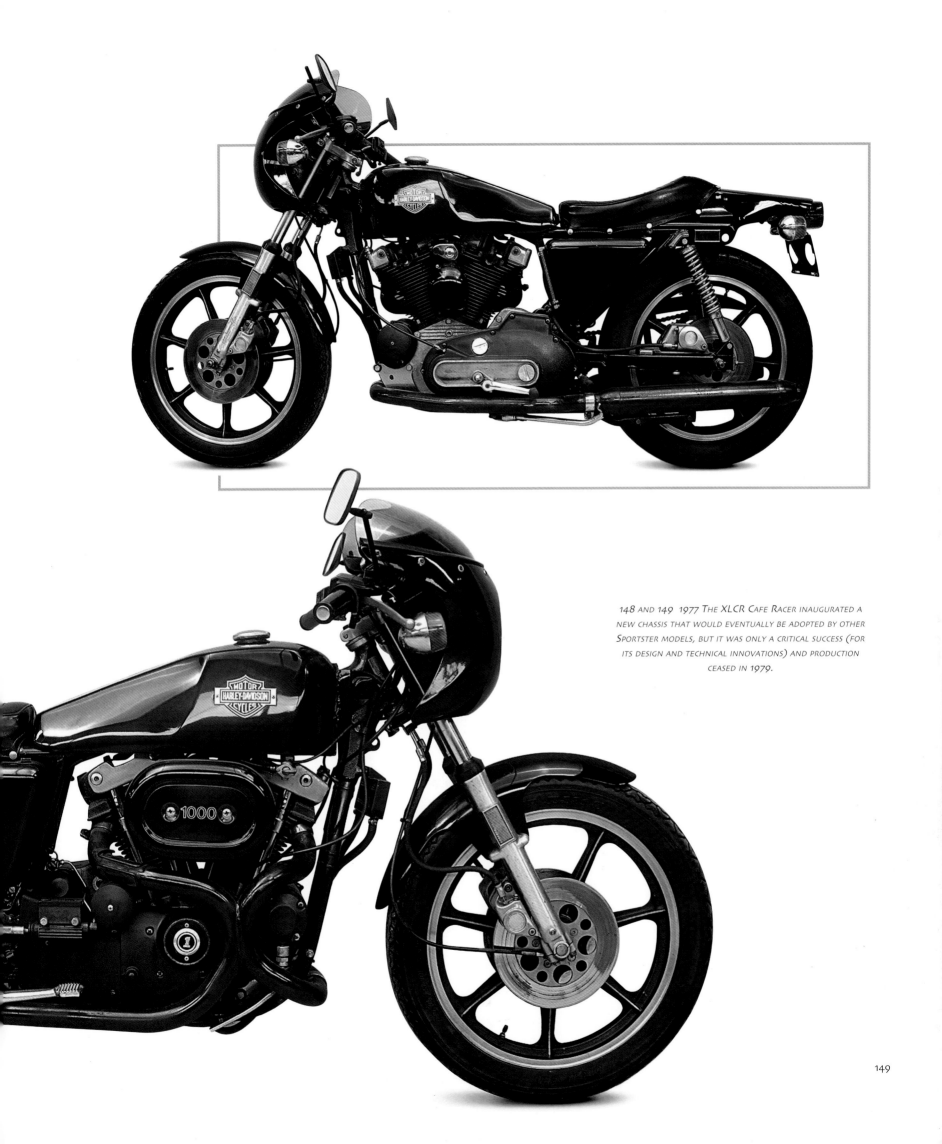

148 AND 149 1977 THE XLCR CAFE RACER INAUGURATED A
NEW CHASSIS THAT WOULD EVENTUALLY BE ADOPTED BY OTHER
SPORTSTER MODELS, BUT IT WAS ONLY A CRITICAL SUCCESS (FOR
ITS DESIGN AND TECHNICAL INNOVATIONS) AND PRODUCTION
CEASED IN 1979.

XR 1000 (1983–1984)

The XR 1000 was a sportsbike derived, at least aesthetically, from the XR 750 competition model. Presented at Daytona during Bike Week 1983, it benefited from a successful and well-timed promotional launch, as Jay Springsteen signaled Harley-Davidson's brief return to "Twin" competition by winning the Battle of the Twins with it.

The XR 1000 used the same chassis as the XLX and the same engine as the XL, but it had new cast-iron cylinders that were capped with aluminum heads. Moreover, these heads were internally prepared and polished by an expert, Jerry Branch. The compression ratio was 9:1 and two 36 mm pump-back Dell'Orto carburetors powerered the engine and delivered 70 horsepower. The carburetors were mounted on the right side of the engine with the exhaust on the left, accentuating the racer styling created by the small solo seat, the 2.2 gallon peanut tank, the generous dual front disc brakes and impressive aluminum rims.

With a meter, tachometer and flashers, it proved, despite its racing apperance, to be a good road bike. Its $6,999 price tag, meanwhile, placed it in the high-end category of motorcycles, since it was only slightly less expensive than a Big Twin Super Glide. Nevertheless, sales were strong. Harley-Davidson was still producing them in 1984, the year it launched the Big Twin Evolution aluminum engines, with the Sportster range still retaining its cast-iron block. The XR 1000's braking system was improved, however, and it was now available in black and orange, in addition to the gray color offered on 1983 models.

150-151 Despite its appearance, which was based on the XR 750, the XR 1000 was derived from the XLX and kept its frame and low engine.

SPORTSTER ALU

XLH 883 (1986–2003, it then became the XL 883 2004–2009)

XLH 883 Upgrade (1986–2003), XLH 1100 (1986–1987)

XLH 883 Hugger (1987–2003), XLH 883 Deluxe (1988–1995)

and XL 883 Low (2005–2010), XL 883N Iron (since 2009)

XL 883L SuperLow (since 2011)

XL 53C (1998, it then became the XL 883C Custom 1999–2010)

XL 883R (2002, 2003 and since 2005)

XLH 1200 (1988–1995, it then became the XLH 1200 Standard 1996–2003)

XL 1200S Sport (1996–2003), XL 1200C Custom (1996–2010, 2011)

XL 1200R Roadster (2004–2008), XL 1200L Low (since 2006)

XL 50 50th Anniversary (2007), XL 1200 XL Forty Eight (since 2010)

XL 1200N Nightster (since 2007)

XR 1200 and XR 1200X (since 2008)

XLH 883 (1986–2003, IT THEN BECAME THE XL 883 2004–2009), XLH 883 UPGRADE (1986–2003), XLH 1100 (1986–1987)

It was in the summer of 1985 that Harley-Davidson unveiled the Sportster 883, with an aluminum engine replacing the cast-iron block.

This Evolution 883 engine used 206 entirely new pieces and 426 components in all for a total of 29 percent fewer parts compared to the cast-iron engine. With the original Sportster, Harley-Davidson revived the model 55, as the new aluminum block used the same bore and stroke – 3 inches (7.5 cm) x 3.81 inches (9.5 cm). Powered by a Keihin carburator, it delivered 45 horsepower. The rocker covers were divided into three parts, which allowed the extraction of the cylinder heads without removing the engine from the frame. Plus, it had hydraulic lifters. The internal parts were advertised as being better balanced and lighter, with a much improved oil flow. Improved performance and reliability reduced revisions and overhauls. The frame, although still based on the model introduced in 1982, was so modified that it had to use a new engine and equipment.

The base model of the 1986 Sportster XLH 883 was offered for $3995, the same attractive price as the 1983 XLX and $700 less than the 1985 XLX. It used the same design, with a solo seat, a small peanut tank, a small handlebar and minimal equipment on the base models of the range. There were 10,348 copies produced the first year, with the XLH 883 and the XLH 883 Upgrade, with a special paint and a more complete finish, available in the U.S. In Europe, the 883 XLH came in two versions, the base model and a two-seater called the Deluxe, which came with passenger footrests.

In 1986, a two-seat Sportster XLH 1100 appeared with bigger handlebars, a larger dashboard, a wide choice of colors and a black engine with aluminum fins. Like the European XLH 883, the passenger footrests remained; however, they were fixed on the swingarm for increased comfort. This XLH 1100 was built on the base engine and chassis of the XLH 883 but with a bore and stroke of 3 inches x 4 inches (85 mm x 97 mm). This generated a displacement of 67 cubic inches (1100 cc) and 62 horsepower. Harley-Davidson also produced a "Liberty Edition" model commemorating the 100th anniversary of the Statue of Liberty.

Despite some minor internal changes, the 1987 XLH 883 and 1100 remained virtually unchanged. A Hugger 883 model appeared and the XLH 1100 version was also available in a special version commemorating the 30th anniversary of the Sportster. However, this would prove to be the last year of production for the Sportster 1100. The XLH 883 Hugger model was lowered with the adoption of a slammed suspension and a thinner seat.

XLH 883 HUGGER (1987–2003), XLH 883 DELUXE (1988–1995) AND XL 883 LOW (2005–2010), XL 883N IRON (SINCE 2009), XL 883L SUPERLOW (SINCE 2011)

The Sportsters, like the Big Twins, adopted new camshaft profiles to modify valve opening times, and the Sportster gained about 5 percent more power in 1988. The Sportster 883 received a new Keihin 1.5 inch (40 mm) carburator, a longer swingarm and a fork with a diameter of 1.5 inches (40 mm) instead of the old 1 inch (35 mm) model. The improved model (Upgrade) became the Deluxe.

In 1989, some internal improvements enhanced reliability by reducing revolutions per minute for maximum power and torque, and extra attention was spent on finishing details. In 1990, the Sportster saw its foam air filters replaced with a paper filter and a recirculation pump was added to its carburetor. Sportster sales were stable and Harley-Davidson worked on increasing its production capacity to meet demand.

In 1991, the Sportster received a five-speed transmission and many internal improvements. New hydraulic lifter blocks were built into the crankcase; the alternator, moved to the end of the crankshaft, delivered more power in low revs; and a new oil pump was installed. And, most importantly, the XLH 883 Deluxe adopted a final toothed belt drive, which required a change in the frame, swingarm, rear shocks and the cover of the gearbox output.

Only minor changes to the Sportster range occurred in 1992 and sales remained stable following a sharp increase in 1991 compared to 1990. The belt drive was popular with users, who pushed to have this type of transmission across the range, and in 1993 Harley-Davidson gave in when the XLH Hugger 883 adopted the final toothed belt drive.

In 1994, the Sportster 883 received a modified electrical system, fuel and clutch cable anchoring, while its frame was strengthened. The

152-153 THE LOWERED SPORTSTER, OF THE HUGGER VARIETY, BECAME THE XL 883L LOW IN 2005 BUT RETAINED THE SAME PRINCIPLE OF SHORTENED SUSPENSION, ADDING A REFINED SADDLE.

154 THE NEW ALL-ALUMINUM SPORTSTER ENGINE INCORPORATED A SIMILAR ARCHITECTURE TO THAT OF THE BIG TWIN EVOLUTION FOR ITS TOP ENGINE.

154-155 THE XLH 883, WHOSE ENGINE BLOCK WAS ALUMINUM, APPEARED WITH THE 1986 RANGE AND REPLACED THE IRON SPORTSTER ENGINE WHILE RETAINING THE SPIRIT OF A SIMPLE AND EFFICIENT MACHINE.

company also adopted the lower aluminum fork crown of the Sportster 1200 and added an electronic odometer in 1995.

Until 1996, the 883 Sportster range consisted of three models in the U.S. and two in Europe; as of 1993, the Deluxe was no longer being imported into Europe. But in 1996, there were still only two 883 models, the XLH 883 and XLH Hugger, sold on both continents. The Deluxe model, meanwhile, disappeared from the American catalog.

The following year, the tank of the 883 and the Hugger XLH was changed to the 3.3 gallon (12 .5 L) tank used by the 1200 models. This was the only innovation in 1997. Harley-Davidson celebrated its 95th anniversary in 1998 and limited the evolution of its motorcycles, content to offer special anniversary paint as an option.

The 1999 XLH Sportster 883 Standard and the XLH 883 Hugger remained virtually unchanged, but they did benefit from some mechanical improvements on the crankshaft, hydraulic lifters, camshaft and oil passages in 2000. In 2001, they gained 7 percent more power thanks to changes in the exhaust and intake. They also received new camshaft sprockets, a new oil pump and Spinylok cylinder liners adopted from the Twin-Cam 88 engine. These would represent the last major innovations before Harley-Davidson's 100th anniversary, as the company then began focusing primarily on production to meet booming demand.

The Sportster 883's anniversary in 2003 was commemorated with the "Rarities" series, while the one-seater XLH 883 Sportster remained the base model Sportster, with a very low and attractive price. The Sportster XLH 883 Hugger was a XLH with a lower suspension and seat to accommodate smaller users and female drivers.

The following year, Harley-Davidson unveiled its 2004 range, which had significantly changed and, in the process, introduced a new generation of Sportsters. This new line, with a recast XL Evolution engine mounted in a 26 percent more rigid frame, provided a lowered seat height and came in four models, with the base model being the XL Sportster 883.

The Evolution V-Twin had been thoroughly reworked for 2004, with each piece subject to a full review. And, while the engine retained the same bore and stroke, its cooling was improved with larger cylinder fins and cylinder heads, not to mention new pistons that benefited from oil jets directed at the underside of the piston.

The power gain came mainly from the adoption of lighter pistons and connecting rods, new large gas flow cylinder heads and higher performance camshafts that improved the torque. These XL Evolution engines also evolved in terms of style, with new two-part rocker covers, primary transmission housings and gear, derby cover (which was a cover on the clutch) and an updated form of the classic oval air filter cover.

The chassis also received significant changes, since the engines were now mounted in silent blocks through a new frame. This replaced the traditional Sportster frame. The system was inspired partly by the Buell, with the motor connected to the frame at three points by flexible rubber mountings. These points were at the junction of the motor and the swingarm. The vibrations perceived by the driver were reduced and comfort improved. The handling also benefited from the new stiffer frame that offered better steering precision. The rear fender was expanded to cover the new 6 inch (150 mm) tire, which replaced the 5 inch (130 mm) tire on the 2003 models. The new brakes were still single front disc, but they reduced the initial braking.

A new model, the XL 883L Sportster 883 Low, entered the 2005 Sportster range by offering a lowered driving position, reducing the XL 883's seat height to 29 inches (740 mm) and the XL 883L's to 27 inches (685 mm). It used the technique of the old Sportster Hugger, with a fork and lower rear suspension, a refined and advanced solo seat, repositioned handlebars and driver footrests that slightly pushed back. Like other 2005 Sportsters, the base remained virtually identical to the 2004 models, with only a

157 THE BASE MODEL SPORTSTER 883 WITH AN ALUMINUM ENGINE WAS CALLED THE XLH AND THEN THE XL. IT REMAINED THE ENTRY-LEVEL HARLEY-DAVIDSON MOTORCYCLE FROM 1986 TO 2009.

new swingarm and increased rear axle diameter to provide superior handling. It was not imported into Europe that first year.

From 2006, the XL Sportster 883L was imported into Europe and all of the Sportster family had a new transmission for smoother shifting. Is also acquired a new clutch that reduced the gear stick action by 17 percent compared to the 883.

The seat height of the XL 883L Sportster 883 Low was lowered by 1 inch (20 mm) and went from 27 inches (690 mm) in 2006 to 26 inches (670 mm) in 2007 with the adoption of new rear shocks and fork springs.

In 2007, the Sportster 883 abandoned its traditional carburetor in favor of a modern electronic fuel injection, but this change was not visible externally. Harley-Davidson also slightly redesigned the frame and remodeled the rear fender, seat, tank, exhaust and intake system. All

block engines of the 2007 Sportster 883 models were also reworked to provide better performance. In addition to the new injection system, a new camshaft helped generate more torque at lower rpm levels, which increased the sensitivity of the throttle and improved performance at 2500 rpm, with a maximum torque that increased from 6.9 daN.m at 4200 rpm to 7 daN.m at 3750 rpm in Europe.

All 2007 Sportsters, equipped with new gauges, including a clock on the odometer and a fuel indicator, an odometer and a trip meter, featured improved driving comfort due to better clutch action (8 percent) and a relaxed brake lever (between 11 percent and 14 percent, depending on the model).

The new Harley-Davidson hands-free security system, which armed and disarmed itself automatically, was standard on all European models in the

2007 range and optional in the U.S. It was the one alarm and security approved by Harley-Davidson and was called the Smart Security System.

Little improvements followed in 2008 and 2009, though all Sportster models did feature a newly calibrated suspension and improved shock absorption for improved ride comfort. The XL 883, meanwhile, was no longer available in America. However, in early 2009 the Sportster Iron 883N was introduced.

The Iron Sportster was raw and minimalist, and as the base model it embodied the spirit of the former XLX. Logically, the XL 883 disappeared from the European range in 2010. And, for 2011, the Sportster XL 883L SuperLow replaced the XL 883 Low. The SuperLow was intended primarily for beginners and smaller riders who were reassured by the 27 inch (695 mm) seat height and the natural driving position.

There was a new entry in the European Harley-Davidson catalog in 1998. The XL 53C was a custom model that adopted the styling of the XL 1200C Sportster, with a full 16-inch (40 cm) rear wheel and a 21-inch (53 cm) front wheel. It was only available in Europe that first year and at an attractive price. Created at the request of its European customers, the 53C XL Custom was released globally in 1999 as the XL 883C Custom, with advanced controls and drag bar handlebars as standard equipment.

In 2000, it was equipped with a 4.4 gallon (17 L) tank in Europe and a year later it benefited from the same mechanical upgrades as other Sportster 883s.

The 2002 range welcomed a new model, the XL 883R, which received an overall racing aesthetic inspired by the XR 750. With its spoked wheels equipped with a four-piston dual disc front brake, wide handlebars, a 2-into-1 chrome exhaust, a fastback seat and inspiration drawn resolutely from the dirt-track world, it called to mind a type of customization that professionals and amateur bikers had been doing since the XLH 883.

The year 2003 was characterized by a Harley-Davidson range totally dedicated to the anniversary of the brand. Sportsters, therefore, were endowed with a commemorative decal on the tank celebrating the 100 years of the company. Only the XL 883R retained its Harley-Davidson sport logo on the tank; however, the 100-year anniversary em-

blem popped up in various other locations, most usually on the crankcase and the front fender.

The Sportster 883R was no longer available in 2004. However, the XL 883C Custom enjoyed the same radical transformation as the base model, including a larger, 4.5 gallon (17 L) tank. The XL 883C, like all other 2005 Sportsters, received a new swingarm and saw its rear axle diameter increase for superior handling.

The XL Sportster 883R, which debuted early in 2005, was a new model equipped with a performance camshaft. It was inspired by dirtbikes and it adopted the orange look of Harley-Davidson racers but with a black power booster and transmission. It was also available in a full black version.

In 2006, the Sportster XL 883R retained its XR flat-track inspired aesthetic but expanded its range of colors to include a beautiful silver. Both the XL 883C Custom and the XL 883R received fuel injection in 2007 in addition to mechanical improvements and new equipment, as did the other Sportsters. These two Sportsters would remain unchanged, except for their paint, for 2008 and 2009, with the XL 883R no longer present in the American catalog in 2008. Then, in 2010, it was the XL 883C Custom's turn to disappear from the American catalog. The XL 883C Sportster Custom also disappeared from the European catalog, even though the XL 883R was still present in Europe.

158-159 *The European model of the XL 883C Custom replaced its small tank with a 4.4 gallon (16.5 L) tank in 2000.*

160-161 *THE XL 883R IN 2002 AND 2003 HAD A TWO-IN-ONE EXHAUST UNDERLINING ITS SPORTY DESIGN. THE MODEL, WHICH RETURNED TO THE CATALOG IN 2005, HAD A CLASSIC SPORTSTER EXHAUST BUT A HIGH-PERFORMANCE CAMSHAFT.*

XLH 1200 (1988–1995, IT THEN BECAME THE XLH 1200 STANDARD 1996–2003), XL 1200S SPORT (1996–2003), XL 1200C CUSTOM (1996–2010, 2011), XL 1200R ROADSTER (2004–2008), XL 1200L LOW (SINCE 2006), XL 50 50th ANNIVERSARY (2007), XL 1200 XL FORTY EIGHT (SINCE 2010)

The new 1988 Sportster was called the XLH 1200 and it replaced the XLH 1100, as the latter's engine capacity, which was deemed too similar to that of the 883, did not help generate enough sales. This was the Sportster with the largest displacement ever produced and it delivered 12 percent more power and 10 percent more torque than the XLH 1100 model, with a bore and stroke of 3.5x3.8 inches (9x10 cm) and 64 horsepower.

The Sportster 1200 for 1989 and 1990 had the same upgrades as the 883 models and received a five-speed transmission in 1991 with the same internal improvements as the 883. Besides these, however, the XLH 1200 also adopted a belt drive that required a new frame, swingarm, rear shocks and cover for the gear box output.

The 1992 modification were minimal and, in 1993, the Sportster XLH 1200 was available in a limited edition series celebrating the 90-year anniversary of the brand. The electrical system, carburetor and clutch cable anchor were amended in 1994 and the frame was strengthened. An electronic odometer was mounted in 1995.

Until 1995, there was only one Sportster 1200, but starting in 1996 the 1200 became a flagship model with the appearance of the XL 1200C Custom, the XL 1200S Sport and the XLH 1200 (which took the designation XLH 1200 Standard) in the U.S. In Europe, the XLH 1200 disappeared from the catalog in favor of the Custom and Sport models.

Based on the XLH 1200, the XL 1200S Sport and XL 1200C Custom were aimed at very different audiences, with one focused on the sports side with a fork, adjustable shock absorbers and a dual floating front disc brake and the other on amateur bikers looking to customize their bikes

with a full 16-inch (40 cm) rear wheel, a spoked 21-inch (53 cm) front wheel and a simple, Spartan look, which lent itself to customization. The following year, changes were limited to the Sportster 1200 Standard (not imported in Europe), which adopted a double seat with a removable passenger side.

The new factory built on the outskirts of Kansas City came into operation in 1997 and was scheduled to begin production in 1998 with the Sportster. Harley-Davidson celebrated its 95th year in 1998 with an Anniversary version of the XL 1200C, while the XL 1200S adopted black cylinder heads and saw its compression ratio go from 9:1 to 10:1 in order to gain torque and power. The Sportster XLH 1200 Standard was again imported into Europe. The XL 1200 C received advanced controls and drag bar handlebars in 1999.

The XLH 1200 remained available in North America but disappeared from the European range in 2000, and the 1200 Sportsters were given some mechanical improvements on the crankshaft, hydraulic lifters, camshaft and the oil passages, while the XL 1200C was equipped with a 4.4 gallon (17 L) tank.

As Harley-Davidson prepared for its 100th anniversary, it focused on increasing production to meet demand. Models evolved very little until 2004, and 2003 was characterized by a line of Harley-Davidsons dedicated to the anniversary of the brand. The 1200 Sportster was endowed with an emblem commemorating the 100 years of Harley-Davidson.

The year 2004 belonged to the Sportster, and by the end of August 2003 Harley-Davidson crowned its anniversary ceremonies with tests on its new 2004 models, including its line of

1200 XL Sportsters consisting of the XL 1200R Sportster, the 1200 Roadster and the XL 1200C Sportster Custom.

The Evolution V-Twin kept the same bore and stroke but engine cooling was improved with larger fins for the cylinders and cylinder heads and new pistons. The power gain came mainly from the adoption of lighter pistons and connecting rods, which raised the maximum rpm of the engine from 5500 to 6000, and new large gas flow cylinder heads and high performance camshafts that also improved the torque. The chassis had the same upgrades as the 883, but the Sportster 1200 Roadster featured a dual front disc. This new model, with its classic profile, wide polished handlebars, timeless tank and dashboard tachometer, was designed as a tribute to the XL Sportster 1957.

In 2005, the only new features were a new swingarm and an increased rear axle diameter for superior handling. The 2006 range welcomed a new Sportster 1200 in November 2005, the XL 1200L Low, which stuck to the XL 883L recipe. The seat was lowered to 28 inches (70 cm), 1 inch (30 mm) less than the XL Sportster 1200R Roadster, and the bike was equipped with a 4.4 gallon (17 L) tank. The 1200 Sportster benefited from a new transmission and a new clutch that reduced the gear stick action by 12 percent.

In 2007, an electronic fuel injection system replaced the carburetor on the 1200 Sportster, which received the same upgrades, modifications and new equipment as the 883. The news of the year, though, was the special edition model celebrating the 50th anniversary of the Sportster. This model, however, was actually just a Sportster with a special 50th anniversary

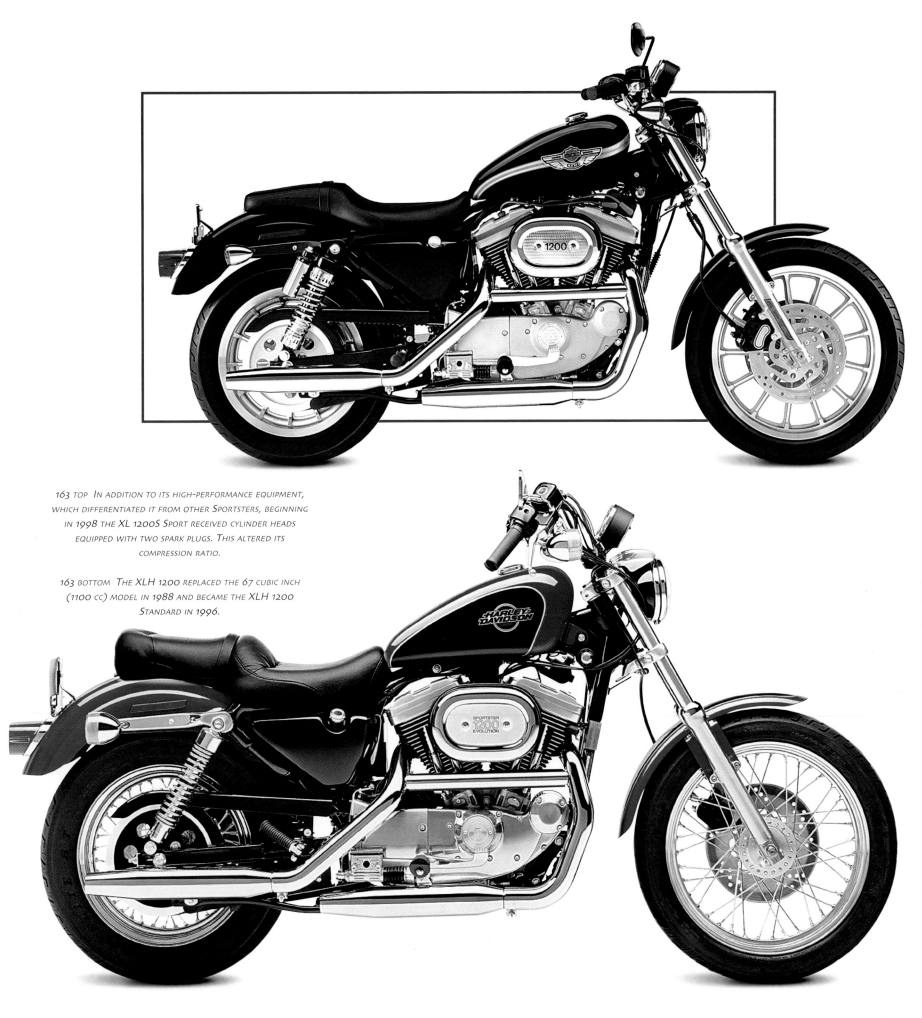

163 TOP IN ADDITION TO ITS HIGH-PERFORMANCE EQUIPMENT,
WHICH DIFFERENTIATED IT FROM OTHER SPORTSTERS, BEGINNING
IN 1998 THE XL 1200S SPORT RECEIVED CYLINDER HEADS
EQUIPPED WITH TWO SPARK PLUGS. THIS ALTERED ITS
COMPRESSION RATIO.

163 BOTTOM THE XLH 1200 REPLACED THE 67 CUBIC INCH
(1100 CC) MODEL IN 1988 AND BECAME THE XLH 1200
STANDARD IN 1996.

logo adorning the traditional 3.3 gallon (12.5 L) peanut tank, a commemorative plaque on the handlebars, a stylized "H" on the lateral sides and a "1957" embroidered in gold on the seat. Available in orange or black, it used the equipment of the XL 1200R Sportster Roadster but with a single front disc. Only 2000 copies were produced in the U.S. in a limited edition.

Limited edition 105th anniversary versions of the XL 1200C Custom and XL 1200L Low were available in 2008 to commemorate Harley-Davidson's history. In 2009, all of the Sportster models received new suspension settings and improved shock absorption, while the XL 1200R Roadster disappeared from the American and European catalogs.

The XL 1200L Low was now only available in the U.S. catalog, while the XL 1200X Forty-Eight was included in the European and American offerings at the beginning of 2010. The Forty-Eight, developed on the base of the Nightster, presented the bobber line with advanced controls and a large 16-inch (40 cm) front wheel. The number 48 was not chosen at random, as 1948 was the year when the legendary peanut tank first appeared. But the Forty-Eight did not rely solely on this tank to stand out, as it came with slammed suspension and a tall and fat 16-inch (40 cm) front tire on a spoked rim that accentuated its squat appearance. The low solo seat, under-mounted mirrors, side mount license plate and clean rear fender also emphasized the Forty-Eight's focus on a minimalist feel.

Following the arrival of the Forty-Eight, the Sportster XL 1200C Custom was no longer available in the U.S. or Europe. But, in early February 2011, Harley-Davidson introduced the new Sportster 1200C Custom, which was completely redesigned, including enlarged triple clamps, 16-inch front wheels and dropped handlebars. It was integrated into both the American and European lines.

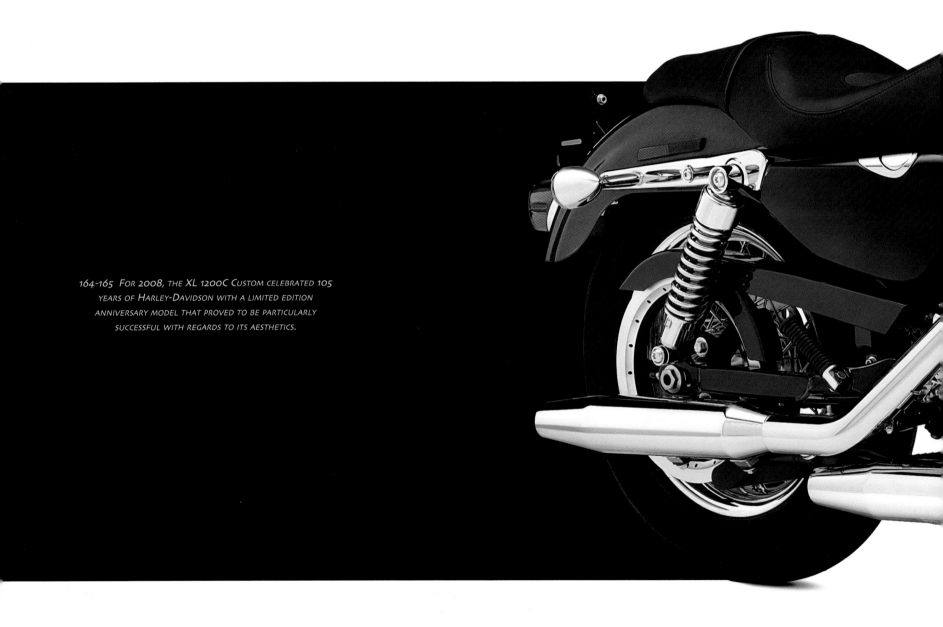

164-165 For 2008, the XL 1200C Custom celebrated 105 years of Harley-Davidson with a limited edition anniversary model that proved to be particularly successful with regards to its aesthetics.

166-167 *The XL 1200R Roadster that appeared in 2004 was actually the new 74 cubic inch (1200 cc) base model, which replaced the 1200 XLH Standard.*

XL 1200N NIGHTSTER (SINCE 2007)

The new Sportster 2007 was unveiled later than expected, joining the American range with the Sportster XL 1200N Nightster in early 2007. The height of the seat was lower than the XL Sportster 1200L Low's 28 inches (70 cm) and identical to that of the XL 883L Low, since it was only 26.3 inches (65 cm) high. Equipped with one seat, semi-advanced controls and wide handlebars, its motor was housed in a dull gray casing and, like its chassis, was decorated in black and chrome. The license plate holder, with light, was located on the rear left side of the bike. The extremity of the small rear fender was given only one reflector, since it was the rear indicators that incorporated the

brake light, position light and turn signals, whereas at the front the fork was given a more retro look and decked out with bellows. By mixing a new unique style with the power and torque of the Evolution V-Twin engine (mounted on a bushing in the frame), the Nightster was well suited to both city driving and touring with an urban underground style that gave this motorcycle a certain spirit.

The new 2008 for Europe was none other than the XL 1200N Nightster. This European version differed from the American model by adopting an extended suspension stroke for improved ground clearance on winding, sinewy European roads and a license plate holder with a light at the rear fend-

er. Like the American version, the rear indicators included the brake light, position light and turn signals. It was, however, still possible to restore the original Sportster appearance by installing a shorter rear suspension available in the Harley-Davidson Genuine Parts and Accessories catalog and to order the lateral license plate holder with a light on the left. Nevertheless, the visually attractive, neo-retro Sportster 1200N Nightster returned the range to its origins. This was a 1200 Sportster with sleek design and a strong visual identity – basically a Sportster stripped down to its bare essentials. In was renewed in subsequent years and offered with different color variations, but it always kept its retro spirit.

168 THE XL 1200N NIGHTSTER WAS STRIPPED DOWN THANKS TO ITS FLASHERS, WHICH ACTED LIKE A BRAKE AND POSITION LIGHT, AND WITH ITS LICENSE PLATE OFFSET ON THE LEFT SIDE.

168-169 THE SPORTSTER NIGHTSTER CREATED A NEW SPORTSTER LOOK AND IT WON OVER MANY WITH ITS LOW AND SLEEK AESTHETIC AND MODERN TECHNOLOGY, WHICH PRODUCED A NEO-RETRO APPEARANCE.

169

XR 1200 AND XR 1200X (SINCE 2008)

The XR 1200 was primarily a simple prototype unveiled in Cologne, Germany, at the INTERMOT Motorcycle Show in October 2006. At that time, Harley-Davidson did not guarantee that it would be mass-produced, as the company first wanted to study and analyze the public and press reactions and comments to determine if the XR 1200 would be as warmly welcomed on the market as it was at shows and exhibitions. As was the case with the XR 1000 in 1983, the XR 1200 prototype sought to use and exploit the legacy of the Harley-Davidson XR 750 racer.

The Milwaukee firm believed that this bike would interest a large portion of drivers who enjoyed sportsbikes, a segment of the motorcycle world that was found primarily in the European market. The study and development of the XR 1200 prototype was therefore conducted jointly between Harley-Davidson engineers in Milwaukee and the Product Planning Europe (PPE) team. The XR 1200, then, had to have a sporty character, so Harley-Davidson enlisted the services of speed bikers for the tests and development of the bike. The aim was to produce a machine that managed to meet the expectations of both European and American drivers, as was the case with the VRSCDX Night Rod Special, which had come from the same collaboration between American and European engineers.

While the XR 1200 was made from a Sportster base, the V-Twin that powered it incoporated technology from the Sportster engines behind the Buell, allowing it to provide between 85 and 90 horsepower. The aesthetics were also updated, with a large volume air box equipped with an electronically-controlled valve discreetly coupled to the fuel tank and two raised exhaust silencers. The suspension system used an aluminum swingarm combined with an adjustable Showa and an inverted fork. Compared to other Sportster models, the ergonomics were decidedly sportier, including repositioned footrests, which were now at the level of the swingarm pivot and on either side of the engine.

Once it passed the prototype stage, and following positive reactions from all corners, the XR 1200 got the green light from Harley-Davidson in July 2007 for a 2008 release. This bike represented a a new marketing approach for Harley-Davidson, which rarely unveils prototypes to the public before deciding if it will actually go to market. Produced since May 2008, the XR 1200 was integrated into the 2009 European line and then to the American line in 2010. However, the bike was criticized in Europe for being too restrained, and by 2010 the sportier XR 1200 X, which was painted black with red stripes, was also available on the other side of the Atlantic. This model received new floating front brake discs and adjustable rear shock absorbers with separate cylinders. Harley-Davidson's 2010 and 2011 European catalogs therefore offered the XR 1200 and XR 1200 X, while Americans had to be content with the XR 1200 in 2010 and the XR 1200 X in 2011.

170-171 *The XR 1200, a Sportster inspired by the XR 750 racing bikes, offered performance and dynamic behavior in connection with its livery. Harley-Davidson designed and manufactured many parts specifically for it, such as the cast aluminum swing arm.*

ELECTRA GLIDE FAMILY

FL/FLH ELECTRA GLIDE PANHEAD ENGINE (1965), FL/FLH ELECTRA GLIDE 74 CI (1966–1980), FLH ELECTRA GLIDE 80 CI SHOVELHEAD ENGINE (1978–1984)

The Harley-Davidson 74 cubic inch (1200 cc) Duo-Glide Panhead engine made one last appearance in the company's catalog in 1965 under the name Electra Glide. This was the 18th year of Panhead production and it would also prove to be its last year of existence. With big wheels and wraparound fenders, a large displacement engine with generous torque and fluid design despite an imposing frame and a large tank, the first 1948 Panheads foretold the spirit of the touring Electra Glide. In 1965, the Panhead engines coming off the assembly lines were mounted on the chassis before being modified to accommodate a larger battery. But these bikes were endowed with one major innovation since the Electra Glide, as its name suggests, had adopted an electric starter system.

Starting in 1966, the Panhead engine gave way to the Shovelhead, which represented a simple evolution of the Panhead. While the lower part of the engine remained unchanged, it differentiated itself with modern and advanced cylinder heads and rocker covers similar to those of the Sportster. It did, however, keep the Panhead's hydraulic lifter distribution system. In view of the important innovations that would emerge in 1970, the Shovelhead generator engine has been baptized the "Early Shovelhead" by some Harley fans, though that designation was never officially recognized by the company. In 1969, in addition to the traditional windshield one could also opt for an Electra Glide equipped with a polyester fairing set on the fork: the famous "batwing" or "pig nose" that is still an inspiration for the fairing of modern-day Electric Glides.

Until 1970, the Electra Glide Shovelhead engine retained the same name as when it was introduced with the Panhead engine, with the "H" models describing high compression. This included the FLB and FLHB models with hand-operated gearshift and the FLFB and FLHFB with foot-operated gearshift (the "B" signified an electric starter). Then, starting in 1970, the FLB and FLHB became the FLH and FLP, with hand-operated gearshifts near the tank. The FLFB and FLHFB with foot-operated gearshifts, meanwhile, became the FLHF and FLPF.

172-173 *The first Electra Glide in 1965 was still a motorcycle powered by a Panhead engine equipped with an electric starter.*

174-175 *To become the Electra Glide, the models of the FL series had to replace their 6-volt battery with a more imposing 12-volt system that required the abandonment of the traditional horseshoe oil tank. A larger oil tank was now positioned on the left side of the bike while the battery was located on the right.*

The 1970 Electra Glide's frame was modified, its generator replaced with an alternator and the Shovelhead engine adopted the aesthetics that it would retain until the end of its production. This engine would remain more or less unchanged on the Evolution model that succeeded it. In 1971, the Electra Glide replaced its Linkert carburetor with Bendix/Zenith models that were supposed to improve performance and, in 1972, it abandoned the front drum brake in favor of a single disc. In 1973, the kickstarter was rendered useless thanks to the reliability of the electric starter and a rear disc replaced the rear drum, but this was not very effective in stopping a bike this big and well-equipped. The 1973 catalog included only the Electra Glide FL and FLH models, formerly the FLHF and FLPF, as the versions with hand-operated gearshifts no longer existed. Always trying to improve its fuel injection, the Electra Glide was equipped with a Keihin carburetor in 1974. Starting that year, the FL was called the police model, with the FLH becoming the reference model. The FLH and FLHF were available in 1974 and 1975, but in 1976 there was only the FLH model that was joined by the FLHS, a limited edition Electra Glide Sport, in 1977.

Harley-Davidson, which had been under the AMF banner since 1969, had no means to counter the modern motorcycles competing with it and the Electra Glide saw no major changes until 1978. That year its engine displacement increased from 74 cubic inches (1200 cc) to 82 cubic inches (1340 cc) and it adopted an electronic ignition and a massive rectangular air filter adorned with a large "80" logo for 80 cubic inches (1300 cc) on the FLH-80 or "1200" for the

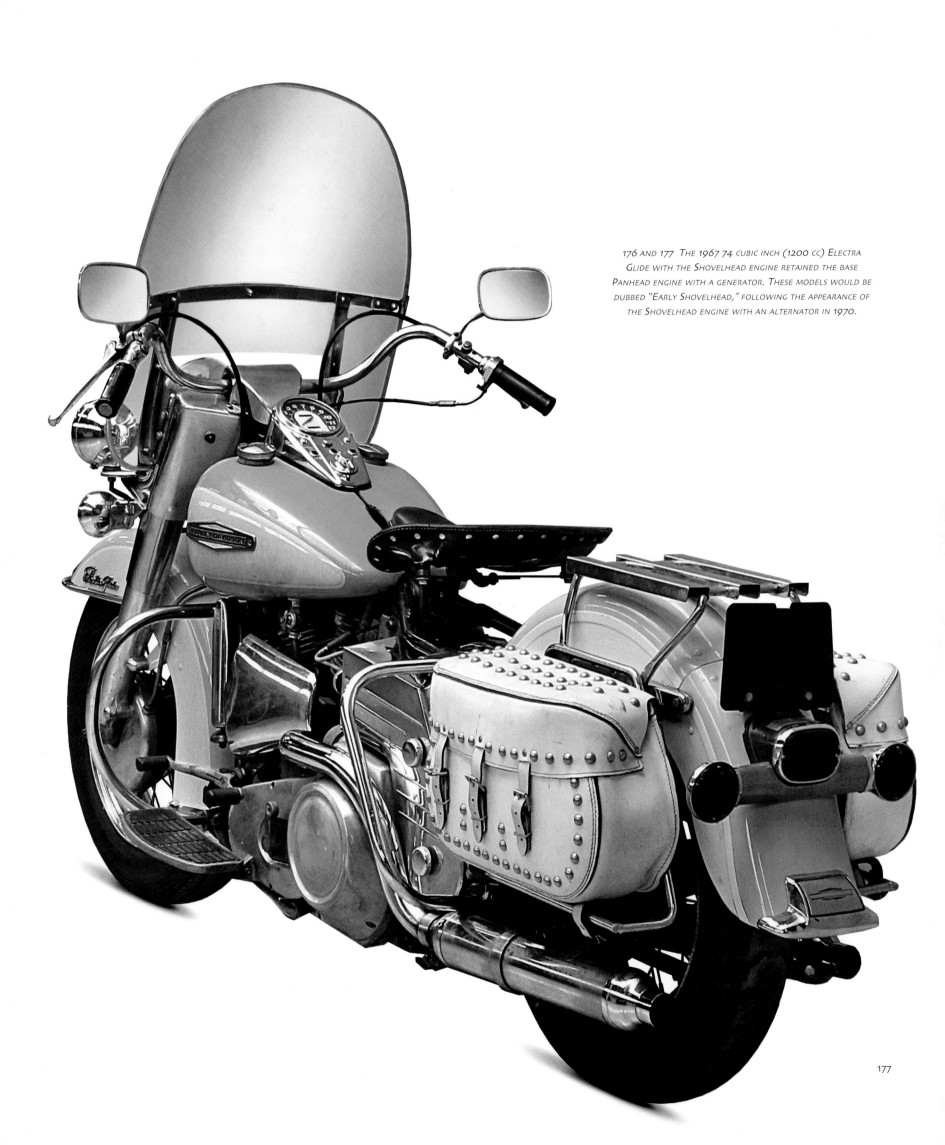

176 AND 177 THE 1967 74 CUBIC INCH (1200 CC) ELECTRA
GLIDE WITH THE SHOVELHEAD ENGINE RETAINED THE BASE
PANHEAD ENGINE WITH A GENERATOR. THESE MODELS WOULD BE
DUBBED "EARLY SHOVELHEAD," FOLLOWING THE APPEARANCE OF
THE SHOVELHEAD ENGINE WITH AN ALTERNATOR IN 1970.

FLH-1200, as the two different engine displacements were present in the catalog.

Beginning in 1979, the FLHC Electra Glide Classic 80 models were delivered with a standard Tour Pak, or trunk. The other Electra Glides of the range that year – the FLH-1200, FLH-80, FLH-1200 Police and FLH-80 Police – did not get this equipment.

In 1980, the FLT-80 Tour Glide appeared adorned with a large fairing attached to the frame in addition to the traditional FLH fairing fixed on the fork. The FLH-80, FLH-1200, FLHS-80 and FLHC-80, meanwhile, received a Motorola electronic ignition with an automatic ad-

vance. The Tour Glide foreshadowed the future Electra Glide with a motor mounted on silent blocks and a five-speed transmission. The 74 cubic inch (1200 cc) Electra Glide engine disappeared in 1981 and the electronic ignition was replaced by the V-Fire II, while the new FLH Electra Glide Heritage model had a retro FLH style with a suspended seat, windshield, leg guards and green olive and orange paint.

The FLH Electra Glide continued its career virtually unchanged in 1982, but in 1983 it received a timing belt. The FLH Electra Glide and FLHS Electra Glide Sport retained their four-speed transmissions, while the new FLHT Elec-

tra Glide and FLHTC Electra Glide Classic were five-speeds and their frames came from the FLT models.

In 1984, both the Electra Glide FLH 80 and the FLHS 80, with Shovelhead engines and four-speed transmissions, were produced for the last time with the FLHX, a "last edition Shovelhead" model with wire wheels and full touring equipment. The FLHTC Electra Glide Classic 80 came with an Evolution engine, five-speed transmission and chain drive enclosed in an oil bath. These then gave way to models powered by an Evolution engine with a secondary transmission belt in 1985.

*178-179 THE 80 CUBIC INCH (1300 CC) 1984 ELECTRA GLIDE
WAS POWERED BY A SHOVELHEAD ENGINE WITH AN ALTERNATOR.
IT STILL HAD THE BIG AIR FILTER BOX INHERITED FROM THE
AMF/HARLEY-DAVIDSON ERA AND WOULD BE THE LAST
BIG TWIN SHOVELHEAD ENGINE PRODUCT.*

FLHTC/FLHTCI CLASSIC ELECTRA GLIDE (SINCE 1984), FLHTCU/FLHTCUI ULTRA CLASSIC ELECTRA GLIDE (SINCE 1989), FLHTK ELECTRA GLIDE ULTRA LIMITED (SINCE 2010)

The four-speed Electra Shovelhead was no longer in the 1985 catalog. The Evolution engine, or "blockhead" all-aluminum, emerged in 1984 and the FLHTC Electra Glide Classic represented a modern evolution on the 82 cubic inch (1300 cc) V-Twin Harley-Davidson block engine. With a combustion chamber benefiting from a new design that enhanced performance, it proved to be both more efficient and reliable than its predecessors and, most importantly, it required less maintenance. It met the expectations of customers and helped rejuvenate the brand, with sales of Harley-Davidson progressing steadily.

The new 1985 Evolution engine on the FLHTC Classic Electra Glide, with a five-speed gearbox and toothed belt drive, would emerge as the standard for all Harley-Davidson GTs to come. Also offered in a "Liberty Edition" in 1986, with the Statue of Liberty represented on the tank and front fender, this FLHTC was joined by a light version, the 1987 FLHS Electra Glide Sport. But, in 1989, the Electra Glide received a few modifications, including a more powerful alternator, and the new FLHTCU Ultra Classic Electra Glide was equipped with lower fairing, cruise control, CB radio and a stereo intercom system between the driver and passenger.

A new 1.5 inch (40 mm) Keihin carburetor with an accelerator pump supplied the Electra Glide engine starting in 1990, and in 1993 a new oil tank was installed under the gearbox. The spot under the seat accommodated the battery, thereby increasing the luggage capacity by 15 percent.

In 1995, a FLHTCUI Ultra Classic Electra Glide celebrated 30 years of the Electra Glide, not on-ly through a commemorative painting but also in its use of injection instead of a carburetor. By 1996 the FLHTC Electra Glide Classic and FLHTCU Ultra Classic Electra Glide were available with either a carburetor or injection system (FLHTCI and FLHTCUI). A new frame lowered the seat height of the Electra Glide family in 1997. In 1998, the Ultra Classic Electra Glide was only available in an injection FLHTCUI version but it also existed as a commemorative model celebrating the 95 years of Harley-Davidson with the Electra Glide FLHTCI Classic injection.

The introduction of a new 88 cubic inch (1450 cc) engine in 1999, called the Twin-Cam 88 or "Fathead," improved the performance, torque and acceleration of the Electra Glide family while still offering a choice between fuel injection or a carburetor. However, the FLHTC and FLHTCI Electra Glide Classic were no longer imported into Europe

In 2000, all Harley-Davidsons had new brakes, a belt drive that was straighter and more solid, a maintenance-free battery and minor internal changes. An original anti-theft system and a new turn signal system improved the range in 2001, and a new electronic diagnostic system reduced maintenance and made repairs easier.

The 2002 models benefited from a new swingarm, suspension and modified frame that provided comfort and better handling. For 2002, the FLHTCUI Ultra Classic Electra Glide fuel injection and the FLHTC Electra Glide Classic (the carburetor version) were imported to Europe, while the 2003 Electra Glide Anniversary Edition was available with commemorative inserts marking the 100-year anniversary of Harley-Davidson.

Starting in 2004, both the Electra Glide Classic and Ultra Classic were only available with fuel injection in Europe, while the FLHTC Electra Glide Classic was still available with the optional carburetor in the U.S. In 2005, the FLHTC was no longer imported in Europe.

The Big Twin was powered by a new 96 cubic inch (1580 cc) Twin-Cam 96 engine with a six-speed gearbox and fuel injection beginning in 2007.

For 2008, Harley-Davidson introduced an anti-lock braking system (ABS) on certain European touring models, which benefited the Ultra Classic Electra Glide. All of the touring models could get ABS, but only as a $795 option in the U.S., and this ABS option preserved the independent front and rear brake systems. In addition, all touring models from the 2008 line were equipped with new Brembo brakes and a 5.9 gallon (22 L) tank.

A new chassis was mounted on the 2009 touring models. The most notable changes included new frames, swingarms, wheels and tires, while the exhaust and engine brackets were also changed. Road holding was the great beneficiary of this redesign. These touring machines also benefited from an increased loading capacity, a more spacious passenger seat, improved protection against heat and more durable tires.

For 2010, the main change concerned the top end of the Electra Glide range with the introduction of the FLHTK Electra Glide Ultra Limited, which came with a 103 cubic inch (1700 cc) engine capacity instead of 96 cubic inches (1570 cc). The engine for this bike proudly bore its displacement on the air filter and distribution cover and offered superior torque for low to mid speeds, all while complying with emission standards. Thus, the value of peak torque went from 13.1 daN.m at 3500 rpm to 13.6 daN.m at the same RPM. In the United States, three machines were available – the FLHTC Electra Glide Classic, the FLHTCU Ultra Classic Electra Glide and the FLHTK Electra Glide Ultra Limited – while in Europe the FLHTC Electra Glide Classic was not imported.

In Europe, all touring models were equipped with ABS and gained some power in 2011 thanks to the Twin-Cam 103 engine, which was standard on the FLHTC Electra Glide Classic and FLHTK Electra Glide Ultra Limited, while the FLHTCU Ultra Classic Electra Glide was no longer available.

In the United States, the FLHTC Electra Glide Classic and FLHTCU Ultra Classic Electra Glide was offered with the 96 cubic inch (1570 cc) engine, while the FLHTK Electra Glide Ultra Limited used the 103 cubic inch (1700 cc) engine with optional ABS.

181 THE FLHTCU ULTRA CLASSIC ELECTRA GLIDES WERE LUXURY MODELS EQUIPPED WITH LOWER FAIRING, CRUISE CONTROL, CB RADIO, INTERCOM AND A STEREO SYSTEM FOR THE DRIVER AND PASSENGER.

182-183 THE 96 CUBIC INCH (1570 CC) TWIN-CAM 96 THAT HAS POWERED THE ELECTRA GLIDE SINCE 2007 HAS A SIX-SPEED GEARBOX AND FUEL INJECTION AND OFFERS POWER AND TORQUE, AS SEEN ON THIS 2008 FLHTCU ULTRA CLASSIC ELECTRA GLIDE.

The Electra Glides were still called FLH until 1980, when a new model called the FLT Tour Glide appeared. The FLT was intended as competition for the comfortable Japanese touring bikes. While the FLH had never really been changed, the FLT, equipped with a new frame and a huge fairing attached to the frame instead of the chassis, marked a real evolution of the Electra Glide.

Indeed, the Tour Glide foreshadowed the Electra Glide's future, adopting a motor mounted on vibration-filtering silent blocks, which made the engine all but unperceivable to the driver. The ride comfort was significantly improved and reliability increased. With this new chassis, the overall geometry of the Electra Glide was redesigned to improve handling and agility at low speed, while the large wheelbase and large front end provided good stability at high speed. The gearbox copied the company's racing motorcycles, going from four speeds to five, and in the process improving drivability. The secondary transmission was assigned to a chain, but it worked in an oil bath under a sealed housing.

The Motorola electronic ignition with automatic feed was replaced by the V-Fire II in 1981 and the FLTC Tour Glide Classic model, which joined the FLT, had a superior finish.

Both models received some improvements in 1982 and 1983, but in 1984 only the FLTC remained and it underwent a change. The Evolution 80 cubic inch (1300 cc) engine and its transmission were now provided by a toothed belt. The FLTC Tour Glide Classic experienced little change thereafter.

It was not until 1989 that something new appeared, with the FLHTCU Ultra Classic Tour

FLTR/FLTRI ROAD GLIDE (1998–2009)
FLTRX ROAD GLIDE CUSTOM (SINCE 2010)
FLTRU ROAD GLIDE ULTRA (SINCE 2011)

184-185 The FLTCU Ultra Classic Tour Glide was an evolution of the luxury FLTC Tour Glide, with notably lower fairing and complete audio equipment.

Glide, a Tour Glide that received, in addition to the new alternator that equipped many Big Twin models of that year, cruise control, a CB radio, intercom, a full stereo system and front and rear low fairings that protected the legs.

A new 1.5 inch (40 mm) Keihin carburetor was offered on both Tour Glides in 1990, which received mechanical improvements in 1991. They also received minor changes in subsequent years. In 1993, the new oil tank was under the gearbox, thus freeing up space under the seat to accommodate the battery, thereby increasing the luggage capacity by 15 percent. The FLTC, however, was no longer in the catalog in 1995, and in 1996 the FLTCU became the FLTCUI, abandoning its carburetor in favor of electronic fuel injection. This was the last year of production for the Tour Glide model, as the FLTCUI was no longer included in the 1997 range.

The Tour Glide's replacement was called the FLTR Road Glide and it entered the Harley-Davidson catalog in 1998. It was equipped with a slightly refined fairing, which was still mounted on the frame, but it did not have a Tour Pak. However, it was available in a carburetor FLTR or fuel injection FLTRI version.

Its 81 cubic inch (1340 cc) Evolution engine gave way to the 88 cubic inch (1450 cc) Twin-Cam 88 engine, with a choice in the U.S. between fuel injection or a carburetor in 1999, 2000 and 2001, whereas it was only available in a fuel injection version in Europe. Beginning in 2002, the Road Glide FLTRI was no longer imported into Europe while it was still available in two versions, carburetor and fuel injection, in the U.S., but then only in the fuel injection version after 2003.

As all of the 2007 Harley-Davidson Big Twins were fuel injection, due to the new 96 cubic inch (1580 cc) six-speed Twin-Cam 96, the Road Glide FLTRI abandoned the "I" to become the FLTR. Like other Harley-Davidson touring machines, in 2009 it received a new chassis, which improved its handling. However, in 2010 the Road Glide FLTR disappeared from the American catalog and was replaced by the Road Glide Custom FLTRX, which had a lower and more streamlined design. This model, however, has never been imported to Europe.

This FLTRX Twin-Cam 96 engine was available, in 2011, with an optional Twin-Cam 103 cubic inch (1700 cc) engine, while the new Road Glide Ultra FLTRU was only available with the 103 motor, standard anti-lock braking system (optional on other models), a Tour Pak and lower fairings. It revived the spirit of the great Harley-Davidson GT, but these models were not available in Europe in 2011.

186-187 AFTER THE DISAPPEARANCE OF THE TOUR GLIDE, THE FLTR ROAD GLIDE THAT REPLACED IT HAD A SLIGHTLY MORE REFINED DESIGN AND CORRESPONDED BETTER WITH THE NEW SMOOTH LINES AND AESTHETIC STANDARDS FOR BIG GT BIKES.

FLHT/FLHTI ELECTRA GLIDE STANDARD (1995–2010)
FLHXI/FLHX STREET GLIDE (SINCE 2006)

In 1995, the Electra Glide range was completed with the FLHT Electra Glide Standard, a lighter bike that would become the base model of the line. It took the traditional fairing attached to the chassis of the Classic Electra Glide, along with its trunk, luggage rack, some of its chrome and the single-tone paint. Like other Electra Glides, it had a suspension system with pneumatic assistance for the fork and rear shocks.

The Electra Glide Standard in 1996 was still using a carburetor, but it received a new framework in 1997 that lowered the overal seat height. Like all of the 1999 Big Twin models, it adopted a new engine, which replaced the Evolution 80 cubic inch (1300 cc) Twin-Cam 88 Model. However, it was still power by a carburetor. In subsequent years, it enjoyed the same improvements as the other Harley-Davidsons in its class but it did not yet adopt an electronic fuel injection system. In 2003, a FLHTI version with Electra Glide Standard injection was available in the U.S., in addition to the FLHT, which was offered in a carburetor version in Europe.

Starting in 2004, European dealers offered only the injection version of the FLHTI Electra Glide Standard, which was still available with injection (FLHTI) or carburetor (FLHT) in the U.S. The FLHXI Street Glide, a motorcycle that only came in an electronic injection version, joined the touring range in 2006. It was a machine that came without a trunk and drew its inspiration from the design of the Electra Glide Standard, though the bike was lower and more equipped.

For 2007, both the FLHT Electra Glide Standard and the FLHX Street Glide featured the new 96 cubic inch (1580 cc) six-speed Twin-Cam 96 engine and were only available with fuel injection in the U.S. and Europe. Then in 2009 they received the new touring chassis at the same time as the other models in the Electra Glide family. The two models were present in the 2010 European range, though only the FLHX Street Glide was available in America. The Electra Glide Standard FLHT disappeared from the European catalog in 2011. That same year, the European FLHX Street Glide was available with an anti-lock braking system (ABS) and a 103 cubic inch (1700 cc) engine, whereas in the U.S. a choice was offered between the 96 cubic inch (1580 cc) and 103 cubic inch (1700 cc) engines and ABS was optional.

188 INTRODUCED IN 1995, THE FLHT ELECTRA GLIDE STANDARD BECAME THE BASE MODEL OF THE ELECTRA GLIDE AND WAS AN INSTANT SUCCESS DUE TO ITS LOW PRICE POINT.

FLHS ELECTRA GLIDE SPORT (1987–1993), FLHR/FLHRI ROAD KING (SINCE 1994), FLHRCI/FLHRC ROAD KING CLASSIC (SINCE 1998), FLHRSI/FLHRS ROAD KING CUSTOM (2004–2007)

The Electra Glide family expanded with the FLHS Electra Glide Sport in 1987. It prefigured the future King Road, as the windshield was easily removed, and it had a simple luggage rack in place of a Tour Pak. Lighter in both style and drive than a Classic Electra Glide, it had the advantage of offering the comfort and handling of a touring motorcycle adapted for everyday use, either for one or two riders.

Like other Electra Glides, it was modified over the years, adopting a more powerful alternator in 1989, having its carburetor replaced with a 1.5 inch (40 mm) Keihin in 1990 and its seat height lowered in 1992 and, in 1993, its last production year, gaining a new oil tank under the transmission.

In the 1994 catalog, the Electra Glide Sport gave way to the Road King. The FLHR Electra Glide Road King was presented by Harley-Davidson as a simple but practical motorcycle, which revived the classic image of the big American custom touring bike. In essence, the Road King was an Electra Glide without a Tour Pak and with a quickly detachable windshield, saddlebags and passenger seat. In 1995 it abandoned the name FLHR Electra Glide Road King and became simply the FLHR Road King.

Starting in 1996, the Road King was available with either a carburetor (FLHR) or fuel injection (FLHRI), and its new frame lowered the seat height in 1997.

The FLHRCI Road King Classic, which appeared in the 1998 Harley-Davidson catalog, incorporated many features of the Road King, like the detachable windshield and headlight cover but with a new two-seater leather seat which allowed the installation of a backrest for the driver. The saddlebags had a leather finish that matched the seat and used a new leather working method that allowed the bags to hold their shape permanently.

To complete the classic aesthetic of the Road King Classic, the wheels were spoked, the tires had a white stripe and a logo was printed on the seat, saddlebags and fenders. It was only available in an injection version in the U.S. and Europe, while the Road King was still available in the U.S. with a carburetor (the FLHR) and injection (the FLHRI). In Europe, only the FLHR carburetor version was offered.

The Road King abandoned its 80 cubic inch (1340 cc) Evolution engine for the 88 cubic inch (1450 cc) Twin-Cam 88 in 1999. In 2000 and 2001, the Road King received some practical and aesthetic improvements; however, these were minimal. The 2002 models benefited from a new swing arm, suspension and modified framework.

With a standard automatic speed control, and the help of larger footrests, the 2002 Road King affirmed its position as a touring motorcycle of great comfort. The 2003 Road King Anniversary Edition was available with color inserts and memorabilia.

A new FLHRSI Road King Custom was introduced in 2004. It was a lowered, rear-suspension motorcycle with wide handlebars that offered the standard Road King motorcycle look. The three Road King models existed in injection versions in Europe, while FLHR and FLHRC were carburetor versions available in the U.S. until 2006.

Staring in 2007, the three Road King models were powered by a new 97 cubic inch (1584 cc), six-speed Twin-Cam 96 engine with fuel injection. While the FLHR Road King Custom disappeared from the American and European catalogs in 2008, the FLHRC Road King Classic received an anti-lock braking system (ABS) in Europe. This was available as an option on all Road King models in the U.S.

The 2009 Road Kings were equipped with the chassis used for other touring Harley-Davidsons that year. Then, in 2010, when both models were still available in the U.S., Europe received only the FLHRC Road King Classic. In 2011, a new 103 cubic inch (1700 cc) engine powered several Electra Glides. In the U.S., the FLHRC Road King Classic came with the 103 cubic inch (1700 cc) engine and the FLHR Road King came with the 96 cubic inch (1575 cc) variation, though both offered optional ABS brakes. In Europe, the FLHRC Road King Classic, the only model imported from the Road King family, had the 96 cubic inch (1575 cc) engine, with the 103 cubic inch (1700 cc) engine available as an option, while ABS was standard.

190-191 THE *FLHR* ROAD KING, WHICH REPLACED THE *ELECTRA GLIDE SPORT*, USED THE SAME PRINCIPLES AS THE *SPORT* BUT WITH A LIGHTER DESIGN AND LOOK THANKS TO ITS DIFFERENT HEADLIGHT, TANK AND SEAT.

192-193 *THE FLHRC ROAD KING CLASSIC PLAYED ON THE NOSTALGIA EFFECT BY REMAINING A ROAD KING, BUT ONE THAT CAME WITH LEATHER FINISHED SADDLEBAGS, SPOKE WHEELS WITH WHITEWALL TIRES AND A DOUBLE SEAT.*

SUPER GLIDE FAMILY

FX Super Glide (1971–1980 and 1982–1984)
FXR Super Glide (1986–1994), FXDB Dyna Glide Sturgis (1991)
FXDB Daytona Dyna Glide (1992)
FXDC Super Glide Dyna Custom (1992)
FXD/FXDI Dyna Super Glide (1995–2010)
FXDX/FXDXI Dyna Super Glide Sport (1999–2005)
FXDC/FXDCI Dyna Super Glide Custom (since 2005)
FXDI Dyna 35th Anniversary Super Glide (2006)

In 1971, the FX 1200 Super Glide represented an original approach. While the big V-Twin remained housed in an FLH frame, the FX inherited a more refined front end from the XLH Sportster and, as an option, a boattail, which was not experiencing success on the Sportster.

The chassis of the FX Super Glide consisted of an FLH Electra Glide frame with an XL Sportster fork and the engine and transmission from the FLH without the electric starter, while the headlights and brakes came from the XLH. However, the new FX Super Glide was not warmly received when presented in 1971. Its exhaust was composed of two long tubes that were joined into a single large muffler on the right side, and the rear boattail, already unpopular with the Sportster, did not fare any better as an option for this model.

Offered with a Sportster-styled fender, sales of the 1972 FX started to take off. In 1973, the FX Super Glide received front and rear disc brakes, a modern "dual shorty" exhaust and a new one-piece tank that reinforced its sporty image.

The FXE Super Glide joined the FX in 1974 and the two models replaced their wire wheels with spoked wheels in 1977. The ignition switch of the two bikes was replaced with an electronic ignition in 1978. The Super Glide FX, without an electric starter, disappeared in 1979 and the FXE Super Glide was only available with the 73 cubic inch (1200 cc) engine in 1979 and 1980.

The 80 cubic inch (1340 cc) engine replaced the 73 cubic inch (1200 cc) version in 1981 on the FXE Super Glide, which received an electronic ignition V-Fire II, like all of the other Big Twin models that year. In 1982, its four-speed gearbox was replaced with a five-speed transmission, while the range was enriched by the arrival of two other five-speeds: the FXR Super Glide II with wire wheels and the FXRS Super Glide II with spoked rims. The main innovation of these two Super Glides was the new, modern frame. Five times more resistant to torsion, or twisting, it accommodated the mechanical part with silent blocks which filtered the vibration of the big V-Twin. This new geometry, which featured a modified steering column, increased maneuverability, and the two bikes were equipped with dual front disc brakes.

The range remained the same in 1983, but for 1984 only the FXE Super Glide was still present, always with the same configuration. However, the FXE Super Glide was no longer available in the 1985 catalog. The Super Glide joined the Harley-Davidson line in 1986 under the name FXR Super Glide but with an Evolution engine, a five-speed box and a secondary chain transmission. By 1987, the chain was replaced by a belt, and in 1988 the Super Glide received a new 1.5 inch (40 mm) fork (like the Low Riders), a new 32-amp alternator and then, in 1989, the 1.5 inch (40 mm) Keihin carburetor vacuum pump that

194-195 The FXDC Super Glide Dyna Custom was a Super Glide that had a slightly more luxurious finish, most notably chrome and two-tone paint.

196-197 The 1971 FX Super Glide was a new model that fell between the large FL and the Sportster. It was offered, as was the Sportster in 1970 and 1971, with a rear "boat tail" option.

equipped the Big Twin range in 1990. It benefited from the improvements made to the Low Rider and Super Glide ranges in 1991, but real innovation arrived with the FXDB Dyna Glide Sturgis. This motorcycle inaugurated a new central beam steel frame that anchored the engine with two silent blocks, or rubber vibration filters. The engine was also slightly repositioned further forward in the frame and tilted 4 degrees forward, which freed up space to house several different components, while the oil tank was installed under the transmission. All black with red streaks, the Sturgis model reflected the spirit of the first model of this type created on the Low Rider base ten years earlier.

Harley-Davidson renewed the commemorative Dyna Glide operation in 1992 with 1700 copies produced in a limited edition of the FXDB Dyna Glide Daytona. Virtually identical to the Sturgis, the Daytona celebrated the 50 years of the Daytona 200 motorcycle race and distinguished itself with a metallic blue and cream paint, numerous chrome pieces, a large handlebar and a second front disc. That same year, the FXDC Dyna Glide Custom, a Daytona Dyna Glide without the "50th Anniversary Daytona" finish, was also released.

For 1993 and 1994, however, the FXR Super Glide was again alone and in its standard, classic configuration.

In 1995, the FXR became the FXD Dyna Super Glide, which was finally given the Dyna frame. However, it had a caster angle of 28 degrees, while the other 1991 Dyna models all had a 32 degree caster angle up until the previous year.

This Dyna Super Glide continued without major changes until 1999 when, like all Big Twin Harley-Davidsons (except the Softail family), it received a new block engine, the 88 cubic inch (1450 cc) Twin-Cam 88 fueled by a 1.5 inch (40 mm) Keihin. It was now accompanied by the FXDX Dyna Super Glide Sport, which came with a black engine, lengthened suspension and a dual front disc.

From 2004, the European Super Glides were only available with fuel injection, and this is what the extra "I" in their name signified: FXDI Super Glide and FXDXI Super Glide Sport. In the U.S., customers could choose between the carburetor or fuel injection.

The FXDC/FXDCI Dyna Super Glide Custom, which appeared in 2005, was actually a Super Glide that had extra chrome. The FXD/FXDI Super Glide was no longer in the European catalog, but it continued its career in the U.S.

The FXDX/FXDXI Dyna Super Glide Sport disappeared from the 2006 Super Glide family, while all the other bikes in this range received a six-speed gearbox and a new 2 inch (49 mm) fork. It was also now only available with fuel injection. The new FXDI Super Glide 35th Anniversary, which was produced in a limited run of 3500 copies, was a model that paid homage to the original red, white and blue colors of the 1971 FX Super Glide. The Twin-Cam 88 engine gave way to the 96 cubic inch (1580 cc) Twin-Cam 96 engine on all of the 2007 Big Twins and both the FXD and FXDC Super Glides benefited from this change. Both models continued without major changes until 2010, but in 2011 the FXD was no longer available in the U.S. and the FXDC Super Glide Custom was the only version sold on both continents.

198-199 THE FXDX DYNA SUPER GLIDE SPORT HAD A DUAL DISC FRONT SUSPENSION WITH EXTENDED SPRINGS.

199 TOP IN 2000, THE DYNA SUPER GLIDE HAD NEW FLAT
HANDLEBARS IN THE STYLE OF THE XR.

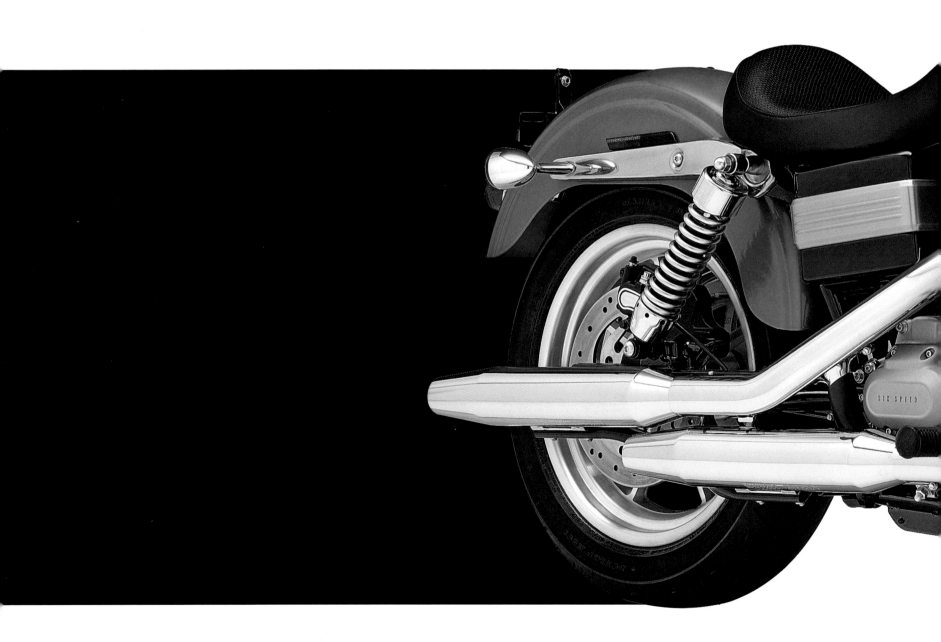

200-201 *THE FXR SUPER GLIDE BECAME THE FXD SUPER GLIDE DYNA IN 1995 BY ADOPTING THE DYNA CHASSIS, AS ON THIS 2008 MODEL.*

LOW RIDER FAMILY

While the first Harley-Davidson FXS Low Rider arrived in 1977, we have to go back to the origins of the Super Glide to really find its roots. The famous 1971 Super Glide gave birth to a whole family of Harley-Davidsons, including the Low Rider, which was seen as a luxury model compared to the Super Glide. The FXS Low Rider used the basic elements of the FXE Super Glide but adopted a more assertive aesthetic character.

The Low Rider was impressive, equipped with a drag-bar handlebar mounted on curved risers, a two-in-one exhaust, three disc brakes, short rear wheel shocks, a 16 inch (40 cm) wheel and a fork with an extended 19 inch (50 cm) wheel, a "Fat Bob" twin tank and metallic gray paint. A monster of raw metal, it stood out as a true custom original. In 1978, the FXS Low Rider was available with other optional paint tones and it received an electronic ignition.

The FXS Low Rider was available with both an 80 cubic inch (1340 cc) and a 73 cubic inch (1200 cc) engine in 1979, like the new FXEF Fat Bob model, which was actually a Low Rider with a wider handlebar and wire wheels. However, in 1980 the FXEF Fat Bob 73 cubic inch (1200 cc) disappeared from the catalog and only a Low Rider kept that engine.

The 1980 FXB Sturgis 80 cubic inch (1340 cc) was a Low Rider painted completely black, with red stripes on its nine-spoke wheels. The fork was extended and, most importantly, the transmission used a primary and secondary belt. In 1981, the FXS Low Rider and FXEF Fat Bob were only available in 80 cubic inch (1340 cc) versions. The FXEF was no longer in the 1982 catalog and the FXRS Low Rider stayed the same. The FXB Sturgis, meanwhile, would receive golden rims, as this was its last year of production.

While the 1983 Low Rider remained un-changed at the chassis, engine and gearbox level, it did adopt a final drive belt and took on the name FXSB Low Rider. Unchanged for 1984, the FXSB Low Rider was accompanied by the FXRS Low Glide, which lowered the suspension to decrease seat height and came with a single front disc, a five-speed Evolution engine and a secondary transmission chain.

The 1984 FXRDG Disc Glide, with an Evolution engine and five-speed gearbox, was a limited edition model based on the FXRS. The FXSB Low Rider finally had an Evolution engine in 1985 with a secondary transmission belt, but it retained its four-speed gearbox, like the Fat Bob FXEF, which reappeared that year. The FXSR Low Glide received a secondary transmission belt. That year, the limited edition model, based on the FXRS Low Glide, was called the FXRC Low Glide Custom and it had spoked wheels, the XR 1000's front fender, chrome and two-tone orange and brown paint.

In 1986 the FXRS Low Rider finally adopted a totally modern configuration with a five-speed gearbox. It came in three models in 1987, with the arrival of the FXLR Low Rider Custom and the FXRS-SP Sport Edition Low Rider. The Custom model was equipped with a 21 inch (53 cm) wire wheel at the front and a solid 16 inch (40 cm) rear wheel, a special tank without a dashboard console and handlebars raised in two pieces where the meter was fixed. The Sport Edition had a lengthened suspension (the length of the former Low Rider) and a dual front disc.

In 1988, the Low Rider received a new 1.5 inch (40 mm) fork and the 1.5 inch (40 mm) Keihin carburetor vacuum pump that equipped the Big Twin team in 1990. It benefited from the improvements made to the entire 1991 Low Rider and Super Glide ranges. In 1992, the FXRS Low

202-203 In 1993, the Low Rider was equipped with the Dyna frame and became the FXDL Dyna Low Rider, like this 2005 model, which is an FXDLI Low Rider because it is equipped with injection.

204-205 The first FXS Low Riders in 1977 and 1978 were very successful thanks to their particularly striking design and imposing mass. They launched a new long motorcycle look, which was low and relaxed.

Rider was no longer present and only the FXLR Low Rider Custom and the FXRS-SP Low Rider Sport Edition remained, though it was no longer available in 1993. In that year, the Low Rider became the Dyna Low Rider by adopting the new Dyna Glide chassis. The Dyna had a caster angle of 32 degrees and was less complex and expensive to manufacture than the former "rubber mounted." Curiously, it also managed to further reduce vibrations transmitted to the driver. One of the most important innovations, however, was the location of the oil tank, which fit under the transmission and not directly under the seat.

In 1993, the FXDL Dyna Low Rider had the new Dyna frame, which had been inaugurated on the 1991 and 1992 Sturgis and Daytona models, while the FXRS-SP Sport edition and the FXLR Low Rider Custom retained their initial configurations with the old frame. However, in 1994 the Sport Edition model was no longer in the catalog, and in 1995 the Custom version also vanished. The next major evolution for the Low Rider was the adoption of the new 88 cubic inch (1450 cc) Twin-Cam 88 block engine in 1999. This engine, combined with the Dyna frame, created a new kind of Low Rider, one that would remain essentially unchanged until 2001, with a lower seat height and a shortened suspension. In 2004, the European Dyna Low Rider became the FXDLI by replacing the carburetor with fuel injection. In the U.S., customers could choose between both options. Like the rest of the Dyna Glide range, starting in 2006 the Low Rider only existed with fuel injection, a six-speed gearbox and a new 2 inch (49 mm) fork. That year, the range was expanded with the addition of the FXDBI Dyna Street Bob, inspired by the "Bobber" spirit, with its ape hanger handlebars. From 2007 on the FXDL Low Rider and FXDB Street Bob received, like other Big Twin Harley-Davidsons, the new 97 cubic inch (1584 cc) Twin-Cam 96 engine. The FXDL Low Rider stayed in the 2009 U.S. catalog but was not imported into Europe. It was no longer offered in the U.S. in 2010, and in 2011 the FXDB Street Bob was the sole representative of the Low Rider category.

206-207 *The 2002 FXDL Dyna Low Rider retained the lowered suspension from the 2001 model, which provided a seat height of 25 inches (60 cm) when the driver was seated.*

HARLEY-DAVIDSON

88 CUBIC INCHES
DYNA LOW RIDER

FXWG WIDE GLIDE AND CUSTOMS

FXWG Wide Glide (1980–1985)
FXDG Disc Glide (1983)
FXDWG/FXDWGI Dyna Wide Glide (1993–2008)
FXDF Dyna Fat Bob (since 2008)
FXDWG Wide Glide (since 2010)

The 80 cubic inch (1300 cc) FXWG Wide Glide, a new model based on the Low Rider, saw the light of day in 1980. It featured an extended Electra Glide fork, mounted with wide-spaced fork tubes and a 21-inch (53 cm) spoked front wheel. With its very low base, its small headlight lost among the wide-spaced fork tubes, the large fuel tank emblazoned with red-to-yellow flames, its advanced controls, big handlebars and Fat Bob rear fender, it was perhaps the truest "chopper" the company had manufactured to date. While other models in the Super Glide and Low Rider ranges evolved, the Wide Glide retained its chassis and its 80-inch (200 cm), four-speed Shovelhead engine until 1984, although, from that year on, it came with a secondary belt transmission. The last 1984 models abandoned the Shovelhead engine in favor of the Evolution engine.

In 1983, the Wide Glide was joined by the FXDG Disc Glide, which was a five-speed Wide Glide with a final drive belt. The last Wide Glides manufactured in 1984 were now equipped with the 80-inch (200 cm) Evolution engine, but they retained the four-speed gearbox until 1985, the last year of production for this version. The Wide Glide made a comeback in 1993 but with the new Dyna chassis. The FXDWG Dyna Wide Glide used the recipe of the old Wide Glide, with its 16 inch (40 cm) and 21 inch (53 cm) rear and front wire wheels and two front discs. For 1995, the Wide Glide abandoned the Dyna range's standard 32 degree caster angle for a 35 degree angle which was more consistent with the chopper philosophy.

In 1999, the Dyna Wide Glide was powered, like the other models in the Super Glide and Low Rider ranges, by the new 88 cubic inch (1450 cc) Twin-Cam 88 Fathead engine. The Wide Glide remained virtually unchanged until 2004, when it received a fuel injection system instead of the carburetor and became the FXD-

WGI. Only available in Europe with fuel injection, U.S. customers could choose between the carburetor or injection. In 2006 the Wide Glide was only available with injection, and it received the six-speed gearbox used by the Dyna Glides and a new 2 inch (49 mm) fork.

The 2007 FXDWG Wide Glide was equipped, like other Big Twin Harley-Davidsons, with the new 97 cubic inch (1584 cc) Twin-Cam 96 engine. With its full perforated rims, two front discs, flat drag-bar handlebar with internal wiring and twin headlights braced between polished triple clamps, the new FXDF Dyna Fat Bob that ap-

peared in 2008 was a motorcycle that displayed a decidedly modern chopper look. The FXDWG Wide Glide, however, was only available in the American catalog.

The Wide Glide disappeared from the American market in 2009, but it was back on both continents, North America and Europe, starting in 2010. Redesigned, the FXDWG Wide Glide was back with an accent on the old chopper style, maintaining its famous flamed tank. Both the FXDWG Wide Glide and Fat Bob FXDF models remained in the 2011 American and European catalogs, with only minor variations in color.

208-209 THE 2008 FXDWG DYNA WIDE GLIDE, WHICH RETAINED THE SAME CONFIGURATION WITH ITS WIDE FORK AND CHOPPER LOOK, WAS ALSO AVAILABLE IN AN ANNIVERSARY MODEL CELEBRATING 105 YEARS OF HARLEY-DAVIDSON.

210-211 THE NEW 88 CUBIC INCH (1450 CC) TWIN-CAM 88 ENGINE EQUIPPED THE FXDGW LINE IN 1999. IT WAS THE LINE'S THIRD ENGINE, WHICH EXEMPLIFIES ITS LONGEVITY. IT HAD, IN YEARS PAST, BEEN POWERED BY THE SHOVELHEAD AND EVOLUTION ENGINES.

SPORT GLIDE
AND CONVERTIBLES

The 1983 FXRT Glide Sport was described by Harley-Davidson as a light touring motorcycle. Equipped with an aerodynamic fairing fixed to its frame, saddlebags, an air adjustable anti-dive fork and a secondary transmission chain, it was made from the chassis of the FXRS Low Rider and had a five-speed transmission.

In 1984, it abandoned its Shovelhead engine in favor of the Evolution block engine, and a second model, similarly equipped, was soon released – the FXRP Police. This model was ideally suited for use by the police and would be mainly marketed that way, as the civilian model FXRT was struggling with the perception that it was "not enough Harley-Davidson." These two bikes received a secondary belt transmission in 1985. The 1986 FXRD Sport Glide Grand Touring model was actually an FXRT Sport Glide model that came with a trunk and a full stereo system. In 1987, the FXRT Glide Sport had the standard stereo system and, like all other models, was given the 1.5 inch (40 mm) fork in 1988.

The FXRS-CONV Low Rider Convertible, which appeared in 1989 alongside the FXRT Sport Glide, was a Low Rider equipped with a removable windshield and leather saddlebags, highway pegs and a small sissy bar. Both models received the carburetor and Mikuni 1.5 inch (40 mm) vacuum pump in 1990, as well as all other technical improvements made to the 1991 Super Glide and Low Rider ranges. The FXRT Sport Glide was no longer in the 1993 range, the last year the FXRS-CONV was available in its original configuration. Indeed, starting in 1994, it changed its name in reference to its new Dyna chassis and became the FXDS-CONV Low Rider Convertible. For 1995, the Dyna Convertible abandoned the Dyna's standard 32 degree caster angle for the 28 degree caster angle on the new Dyna Super Glide, which increased maneuverability.

This Dyna Convertible remained in the Harley-Davidson catalog without major changes until 1999 when it adopted, like other Dynas, the new 88 cubic inch (1450 cc) Twin-Cam 88 engine, which replaced the Evolution engine. But that same year, the FXDS-CONV would not be imported into Europe and would only be available in the U.S. In 2001, the FXDS-CONV was replaced by the FXDST, while the Dyna Super Glide T-Sport was also imported into Europe. This bike had an adjustable small fairing and removable windshield, a pair of expandable nylon saddlebags and a fully adjustable suspension. It was renewed in 2002 and 2003, but by 2004 it was no longer part of the Harley-Davidson catalog.

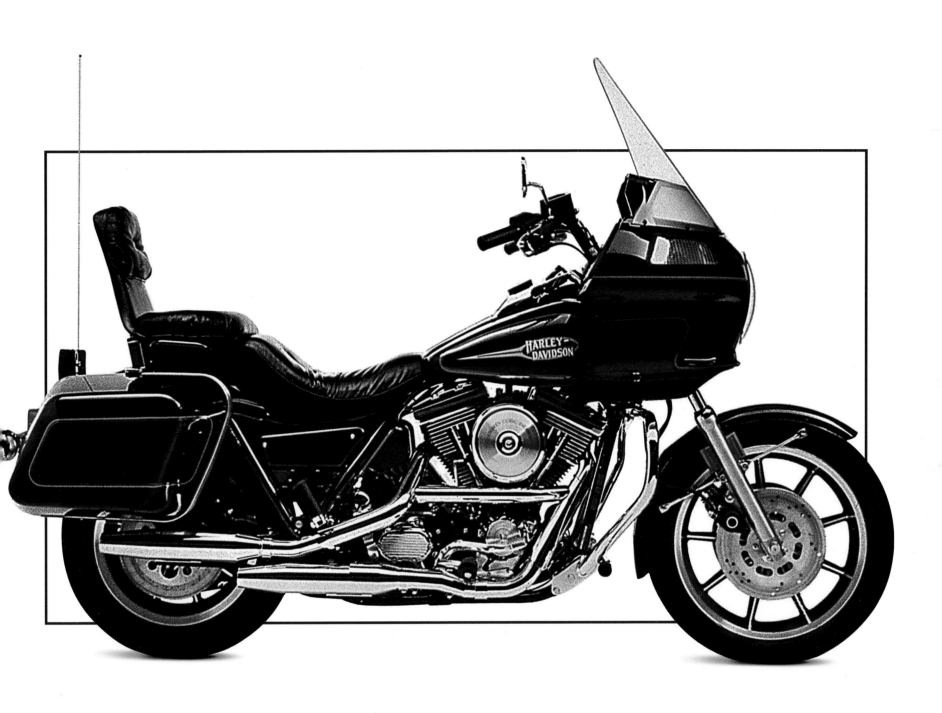

SOFTAIL STANDARD AND CUSTOMS

FXST Softail (1984–1990)

FXSTC Softail Custom (1986–1998) (2007–2010)

FXSTB/FXSTBI Night Train (1998–2009)

FXST/FXSTI Softail Standard (1999–2007)

FXSTD/FXSTDI Softail Deuce (2000–2007)

FXCW Rocker (2008–2009)

FXCWC Rocker C (since 2008)

FXS Blackline (since 2011)

The Softail and the aluminum Evolution engine were intimately linked to the revival of Harley-Davidson. In 1984, when the Milwaukee firm had regained its independence, these two major innovations symbolized the brand's rebirth. The 80 cubic inch (1340 cc) V2 Evolution engine would gradually replace the Shovelhead engine that propelled "the bike from Milwaukee" into the modern era. The vibrations were still there but only for the amusement of Softail drivers, as the Electra Glide, Low Rider and Dyna Glide ranges saw their engine mounted to the frame on vibration-filtering rubber silent blocks.

The FXST Softail, inspired by the very "chopper-esque" look of the Wide Glide with a 16-inch (40 cm) rear wheel and a 21-inch (53 cm) front wheel, married modern technology and nostalgic design. Its new frame had a rear end similar to motorcycles with more rigid frames and was seemingly without shocks, just like

motorcycles from the 1950s. In fact, however, the shocks were hidden under the gearbox. This first 1984 FXST Softail was powered by the new aluminum 80 cubic inch (1340 cc) Evolution engine; however, it had a four-speed box and a secondary chain transmission.

Unchanged in 1985, it evolved and multiplied in 1986. New models emerged and created a whole range around the chassis, and the Softail family adopted a five-speed transmission and a secondary timing belt.

In 1986, the FXSTC Softail Custom differentiated itself from the FXST Softail with a forged aluminum rear wheel, a sissy bar, a black engine, chrome (aluminum on the Softail) and a stylized Harley-Davidson logo. In a few years' time, this Custom model would cannibalize Softail sales.

The forks on all of the 1988 Softails were changed to 1.5 inches (40 mm) in diameter and, in 1989, the Softail range received some electri-

cal improvements (a more powerful alternator) and mechanical changes (a new solenoid shift starter system). The new rear shock absorbers abandoned the separate cylinder system and managed 23 percent more load and 22 percent more clearance.

In 1990, like all Big Twin Harley-Davidsons, the Softail line was powered by a new 1.5 inch (40 mm) Keihin. The relatively low Softail sales compared to the Softail Custom model led to the removal of this model from the 1991 catalog, and the Softail Custom benefited from continous minor mechanical improvements. These changes would continue until 1998.

The FXSTB Night Train appeared in 1998. It was designed on the base of a Softail Custom and was entirely black. It was only intended for the European market; however, its attractive price earned it immediate success and Harley-Davidson released it globally in 1999. In the same spirit, Harley-Davidson reintroduced a

216-217 THE FXST SOFTAIL STANDARD, THE BASE MODEL IN THIS CATEGORY, REPLACED THE SOFTAIL CUSTOM IN 1999 AND REMAINED IN THE HARLEY-DAVIDSON CATALOG UNTIL 2007.

218-219 WITH THE FXSTD SOFTAIL DEUCE, HARLEY-DAVIDSON OFFERED A SOFTAIL MODEL WITH A MORE TRADITIONAL AESTHETIC BY MIXING STYLES.

219 TOP *THE 81 CUBIC INCH (1300 CC) EVOLUTION ALUMINUM ENGINE REPLACED THE IRON SHOVELHEAD BLOCK ON SEVERAL MODELS IN 1984 AND ALL BIG TWINS IN 1985.*

220-221 THE REAR FENDER OF THE FXCWC ROCKER
WAS FIXED TO THE SWINGARM, ALLOWING IT TO STICK
AS CLOSE TO THE WIDE REAR TIRE AS POSSIBLE.
THE SMALL REAR PASSENGER SEAT WAS REMOVABLE.

base Softail, the FXST Softail Standard, which was also very attractively priced. This model took the place of the Softail Custom, which disappeared from the catalog in 1999.

In 2000, the Softail line switched to the 88 cubic inch (1450 cc) Twin-Cam 88B engine, which had been adopted by the brand's Big Twins the year before. It also adopted a new frame to accommodate the engine change. In addition, the Twin-Cam 88B featured a double rocker internal balancing system that further reduced vibrations. The whole Softail range would also benefit from many mechanical and aesthetic improvements.

The range was enriched in 2000 with a new model, the FXSTD Softail Deuce, which came with a wide 17-inch (43 cm) rear wheel, and whose refined, streamlined styling featured an elongated tank.

From 2001, all of the Softails in the American range were available with injection or a carburetor. In Europe, the Softail Deuce had the

same option, while the Standard and Night Train models were only available with a carburetor. For 2002 and 2003 the Softails retained the same configuration and were content to celebrate the 100th anniversary of the brand with a set of special logos in 2003.

In 2004, the FXSTI Softail Standard, FXSTBI Night Train and FXSTDI Deuce were only available with injection in Europe and with either a carburetor or injection in the U.S. These three models were unchanged for 2005 in the U.S., while the Softail Deuce was no longer available in Europe.

Harley-Davidson renewed its block engine in 2007 by introducing the 97 cc (1584 cc) Twin-Cam 96B with standard electronic fuel injection on all of its Big Twin models. This new Twin-Cam improved acceleration and was gentler, even at higher speeds. Gear changes were also facilitated with a flexible clutch.

The new Harley-Davidson hands-free security system, which armed and disarmed automatically, was also standard on all of the 2007 Europeans models and was optional in the U.S. The FXSTC Softail Custom made its return, and while the Softail Standard remained in the American catalog, it was no longer available in Europe.

In 2008, Harley-Davidson celebrated 105 years of existence. The FXSTC Softail Custom, like seven other Harley-Davidsons, came with a "105th Anniversary" limited edition package.

This consisted of two-tone copper and vivid black paint, an air filter box and a decorative saddle, among other special features.

After having disappeared from the European range, the Softail Deuce and Standard would soon vanish from the 2008 Harley-Davidson U.S. catalog as well, with two radical new models taking their places. These were the FXCW Rocker and FXCWC Rocker C, whose rear had adopted a real chopper style, with an enormous 9 inch (240 mm) tire housed in a Softail frame seemingly devoid of suspension thanks to a long fuel tank and an increased caster angle. This tire was topped by a wraparound fender, named the "Rockertail," which was fixed directly to the swingarm without visible support. The Rocker had only a solo saddle, while the Rocker C featured a removable passenger seat that attached to a support bearing on the driver seat. The range remained unchanged in 2009.

In 2010, the FXSTB Night Train and FXCW Rocker were no longer available, and the FXSTC Softail Custom was only part of the the U.S. range. In 2011, only the FXCWC Softail Rocker C, with an anti-lock braking system in Europe and optional ABS in the United States, remained. But, at the beginning of 2011, Harley-Davidson introduced a new Softail, the FXS Blackline, which was closer in spirit to the old chrome Night Train, with a dashboard now placed on the upper fork.

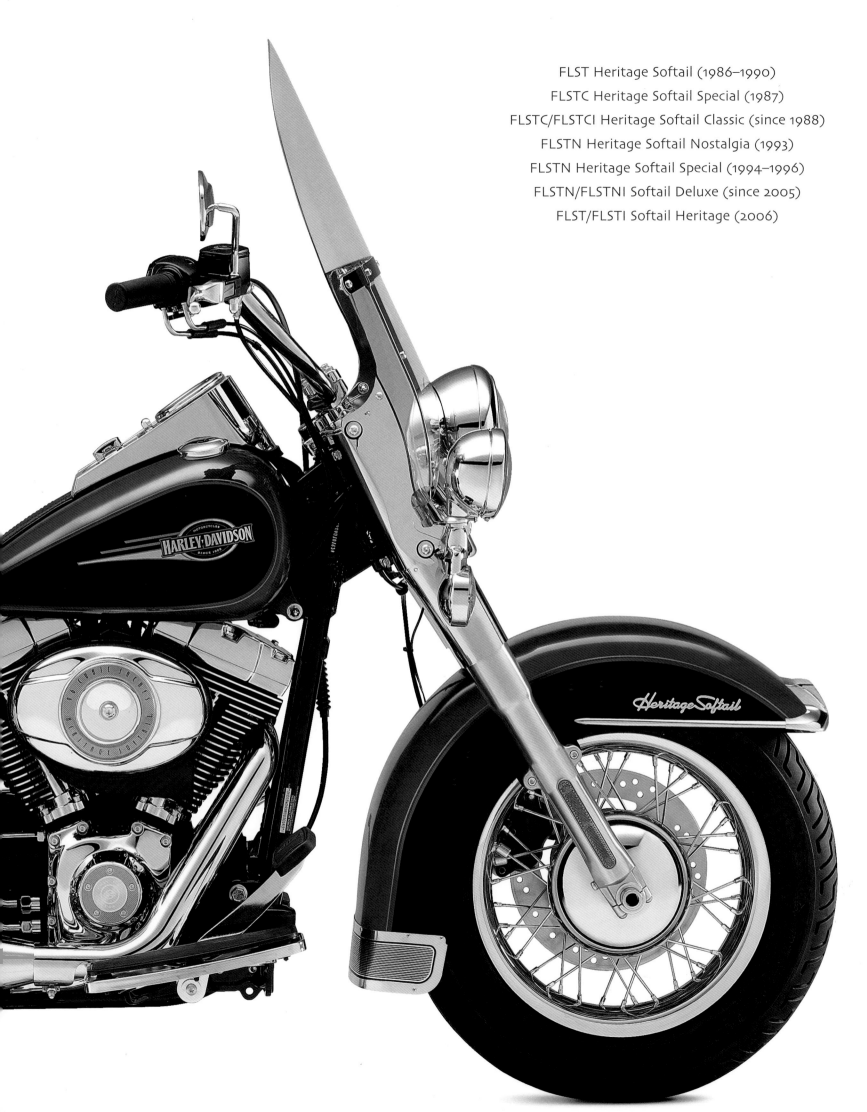

FLST Heritage Softail (1986–1990)

FLSTC Heritage Softail Special (1987)

FLSTC/FLSTCI Heritage Softail Classic (since 1988)

FLSTN Heritage Softail Nostalgia (1993)

FLSTN Heritage Softail Special (1994–1996)

FLSTN/FLSTNI Softail Deluxe (since 2005)

FLST/FLSTI Softail Heritage (2006)

222-223 THE FLSTC HERITAGE SOFTAIL CLASSIC WAS A SOFTAIL
HERITAGE EQUIPPED WITH A WINDSHIELD, LEATHER SADDLEBAGS,
A COMFORTABLE SEAT AND A SISSY BAR, A FORMULA THAT
REMAINED THE SAME OVER THE YEARS, AS IN THE 2008 MODEL.

224 THIS 1987 FLSTC HERITAGE SOFTAIL SPECIAL BEGAN ITS
CAREER AS A LIMITED EDITION MODEL, BUT AFTER 1988 IT WAS
INCORPORATED INTO THE RANGE FOLLOWING ITS INCREDIBLE
SUCCESS UNDER THE FLSTC HERITAGE SOFTAIL CLASSIC NAME.

n the spring of 1986, the FLST Heritage Softail model found wide success. It was the combination of a Softail frame with the front end of an Electra Glide and was a motorcycle that evoked the aesthetics of the 1950s era Hydra Glide. The Heritage model notably featured a big round headlight, wraparound fenders, alloy fork elements and footrests. It retook the name FLH Electra Glide Heritage and adopted the retro FLH styling. It was equipped with fringed saddlebags, a windshield and leg guards.

The Heritage Softail model gave rise in 1987 to a limited series, the FLSTC Heritage Softail Special, which turned into the FLSTC Heritage Softail Classic in 1988. The base was the same as the Heritage Softail without the equipment, and the Special and Classic models were equipped with a windshield, leather saddlebags, a two-part saddle, passing lamps and the black aluminum Heritage engine that was chrome on the Special and the Classic.

The Heritage Softail, like the rest of the 1988 and 1989 Softail range, received mechanical and electrical improvements and the new Keihin carburetor in 1990. The FLST Heritage Softail disappeared from the range in 1991, while the FLSTC Heritage Softail Classic experienced some minor mechanical improvements in 1991, 1992 and 1993.

Harley-Davidson celebrated its 90th anniversary in 1993 and released, in addition to limited edition commemorative models, the FLSTN Heritage Softail Nostalgia, produced on a Heritage Softail base and outfitted with "cow skin" black-and-white whitewall tires and Fat Boy exhausts. Two thousand two hundred copies were produced in a limited edition. Meeting with success, the Nostalgia was integrated into the range in 1994 under the name FLSTN Heritage Softail Special, dropping the cowhide theme and integrating new colors. Up to 1996, minor changes and improvements were made to these two models. In 1997, the FLSTN Heritage Softail Special was no longer, with only the FLSTC Heritage Softail Classic receiving minor changes until 1999.

For 2000, the Heritage Softail was equipped with the new Twin-Cam 88B engine and a new frame. It also underwent the changes and mechanical and aesthetic improvements made on the whole Softail family.

From 2001, the Heritage Softail Classic was available with a carburetor (FLSTC) or electronic fuel injection (FLSTCI). For 2002 and 2003, the Heritage Softail Classic retained the same settings and was content to celebrate the 100th anniversary of the brand with commemorative logos in 2003. In 2004, the FLSTCI Heritage Softail Classic was only available in Europe with fuel injection and with a carburetor or fuel injection in the U.S.

The Softail family finally had a new model in 2005 – the FLSTN/FLSTNI Softail Deluxe. This was a nod to the Harley-Davidsons of old, with a front fork and paint inspired by the 1939 models.

A new model, the FLST/FLSTI Heritage Softail was reintegrated in the American and European lines, but only for 2006. The new 97 cubic inch (1584 cc) Twin-Cam 96B engine with fuel injection powered all Softail models from 2007 on. For 2008, the FLSTC Heritage Softail Classic was available with the "105th Anniversary" limited edition package. The FLSTN Softail Deluxe was not in the 2009 or 2010 European catalog, but it returned in 2011. For 2011, the FLSTC Heritage Classic and FLSTN Deluxe were equipped with a standard anti-lock braking system in Europe and optional ABS in the U.S.

SOFTAIL WITH SPRINGER FORK

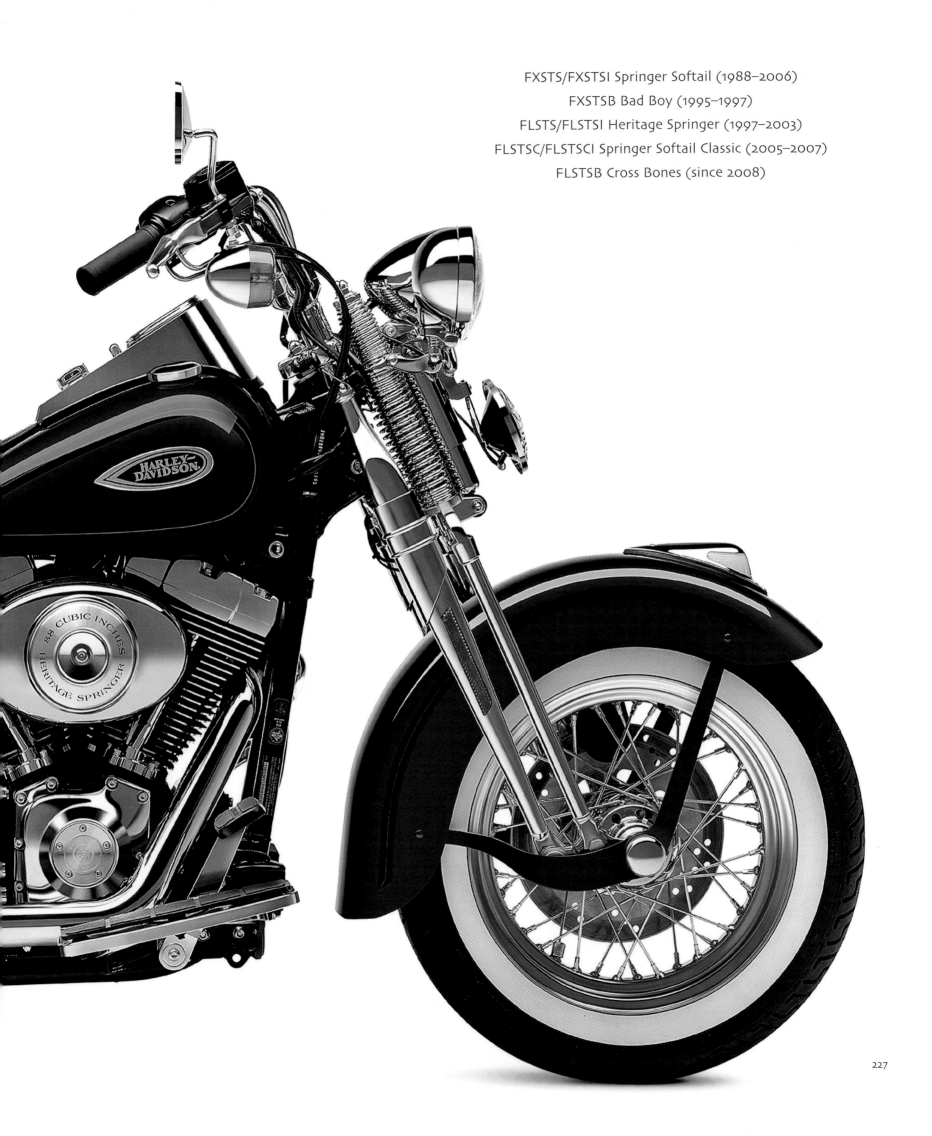

FXSTS/FXSTSI Springer Softail (1988–2006)
FXSTSB Bad Boy (1995–1997)
FLSTS/FLSTSI Heritage Springer (1997–2003)
FLSTSC/FLSTSCI Springer Softail Classic (2005–2007)
FLSTSB Cross Bones (since 2008)

The big news in 1988 was the FXSTS Springer Softail, which was introduced in the middle of the year to commemorate Harley-Davidson's 85th anniversary. This policy allowed the Milwaukee firm to test the market, producing a small quantity of 1,356 Springer Softails with a parallelogram fork. The success of this bike, which offered a retro feel thanks to this fork, was designed with computer-aided techniques that met modern constraints and surpassed all expectations. The Springer Softail still remained in the range.

The Springer Softail received, like the rest of the 1989 Softail family, electrical and mechanical improvements and a new Keihin carburetor in 1990. In 1991, 1992 and 1993 the Springer Softail stayed relatively the same, undergoing only minor mechanical improvements. In fact, the FXSTS Springer changed very little at all, benefiting only from changes made to all Softail models. However, in 1995, with the introduction of the FXSTSB Bad Boy, the Springer was no longer alone. Built on the base of a Springer, the Bad Boy had a slotted rear wheel and a black tint for its Springer fork, oil tank and engine. It was decked out in chrome in 1996, though it still retained the "all-terrain" handlebar that confused most Harley-Davidson customers.

The new FLSTS Heritage Springer, which appeared in 1997, was the most successful copy aesthetically of the 1948 Harley-Davidson Panhead. Nicknamed Ol' Boy, it was equipped with a Springer fork that held a large fender enveloping a 16-inch (40 cm) front wheel, whitewall tires and a saddle that was fringed to match the impressive leather saddlebags. But it was its exhaust system, which featured long mufflers that reached the rear wheel on each side, that truly innovated. The Bad Boy, however, disappeared from the 1998 catalog, as the company offered a limited edition Heritage Springer, with special paint and graphics, to celebrate its 95th anniversary.

The FXSTS Springer Softail and the FLSTS Heritage Springer were equipped with a new 88 cubic inch (1450 cc) Twin-Cam 88B engine and a new frame in 2000, and also given the mechanical and aesthetic improvements enjoyed by the whole Softail family.

Starting in 2001, the FXSTS Springer Softail and the FLSTS Heritage Springer were available with carburetor or electronic fuel injection (FXSTSI or FLSTSI) in the U.S., while they were only available with a carburetor in Europe. For 2002 and 2003, the Springer Softail and the Heritage Springer were left unchanged, with the brand celebrating its 100th anniversary with special logos in 2003. In 2004, the Heritage Softail Springer disappeared, while the FXSTSI Springer was only offered with fuel injection in Europe. In the U.S., however, customers could choose between having it with either a carburetor or fuel injection.

The new 2005 FLSTSCI Springer Softail Classic revived the late 1940s Harley-Davidson spirit

226-227 THE FLSTS HERITAGE SPRINGER, NICKNAMED "OL' BOY," ADOPTED A RETRO LOOK WITH ITS LARGE FRONT WHEEL AND WRAPAROUND FENDER, WHITEWALL TIRES, SADDLE AND FRINGED LEATHER BAGS.

228-229 THE FIRST FXSTS SPRINGER SOFTAIL, WHICH APPEARED WITH THE 1988 RANGE AND REMAINED IN THE CATALOG UNTIL 2006, BROUGHT BACK THE DAYS OF THE OLD SPRINGER FORK.

229

with its wide handlebars, black Springer fork and old Heritage Springer exhaust. From that year on, the FXSTS/FXSTSI Springer would no longer be imported into Europe; however, it remained in the American catalog. The new 97 cubic inch (1584 cc) fuel injection Twin-Cam 96B engine was featured on the only model with a Springer fork, the 2007 FLSTSC Springer Softail Classic, as the FLSTS Springer had just left the American line.

The FLSTSC Springer Softail Classic was no longer in the 2008 catalog, but the FLSTSB Cross Bones took its place in 2008. Its 1950s-inspired bobber look was highlighted by its black Springer fork, ape hanger handlebars and a seat mounted on springs. It was available throughout 2009, 2010 and 2011.

230 top The FLSTB Cross Bones, a Springer model with a strong personality, reclaimed the aesthetic, and especially the spirit, of the bobber-styled motorcycles from the 1950s with its black finish, ape hanger handlebar and solo spring seat.

230-231 From 2005 to 2007, the FLSTSC Softail Springer Classic reclaimed the spirit of the old FLSTS Heritage Springer, without the saddlebags and whitewall tires, but with a black fork.

SOFTAIL FAT BOY

FLSTF/FLSTFI Fat Boy (since 1990)
FLSTFB Fat Boy Lo (Fat Boy Special in Europe) (since 2010)

In 1990, the Softail range expanded with a sixth model, the FLSTF Fat Boy. With its frame painted the same color as its engine, it was based on the Heritage Softail, though it had abandoned spoked wheels for slotted wheels and adopted less enveloping fenders. It was only available in a metallic gray color with a straight shotgun-type exhaust.

By modernizing the retro styling of a Softail, the Fat Boy was an innovation for Harley-Davidson since the massive and imposing appearance of the Fat Boy contrasted with the rest of the Softail line. By 1991, the FLSTF Fat Boy had adopted a more conventional configuration, acquiring a black frame and a black and chrome engine. Over the next eight years the Fat Boy would undergo the same minor improvements as the rest of the Softail family. For the 95th anniversary of Harley-Davidson in 1998, a limited edition Fat Boy was offered with special paint and graphics.

In 2000, the Fat Boy received, like the other Softails, a new 88 cubic inch (1450 cc) Twin-Cam 88B engine and a new frame. The exhaust system was redesigned to improve the view of the engine, and the Softail range was modernized with a new tank, repositioned shock absorbers and, especially, a belt drive that allowed the mounting of a larger rear wheel, which gave the Fat Boy a unique look.

From 2001 on, the Fat Boy was available with a carburetor (FLSTF) or electronic fuel injection (FLSTFI). This stayed the same in 2002 and 2003, with the company commemorating its 100th anniversary with special logos in 2003.

In 2004, the FLSTFI Fat Boy was only available in Europe with fuel injection, while customers in the U.S. could still choose to have it with a carburetor. At the beginning of 2005, Harley-Davidson produced a limited edition model that commemorated the 15-year history of the Fat Boy. However, this silver model emblazoned with the first Fat Boy logo kept a black frame. It was only available in the American market.

The new 97 cubic inch (1584 cc) Twin-Cam 96B engine with fuel injection was used for all Fat Boys starting in 2007. For 2008, the FLSTF Fat Boy was available with the "105th Anniversary" limited edition package. The Fat Boy finally saw a true new version in 2010 with the FLSTFB Fat Boy Lo (called the Special in Europe), which adopted numerous, mostly visual, changes. It had a matte finish, shotgun exhaust, different handlebars and a straighter seat that lowered the height by a half inch (10 mm) – 26.5 inches (680 mm) versus 27 inches (690 mm) on the Fat Boy. These changes reinforced its perceived massiveness. In 2011, the two Fat Boys were offered with a standard anti-lock braking system (ABS) in Europe and optional ABS in the U.S.

232-233 THE FLSTFB FAT BOY LO POSSESSES A SLIGHTLY MORE STREAMLINED PROFILE AND A REDUCED SEAT HEIGHT COMPARED TO THE BASE FAT BOY MODEL.

234 THE ALUMINUM EVOLUTION ENGINE OF THE 1990 FAT BOY IS ADORNED WITH YELLOW ROCKER SUPPORTS, WHICH ENLIVENS THE SILVER-GRAY COLOR OF THE ENTIRE MOTORCYCLE.

237 TOP THE FLSTF FAT BOY REMAINED IN THE HARLEY-
DAVIDSON CATALOG AFTER 1990, BUT THE MODEL IN FOLLOWING
YEARS WOULD RECEIVE A BLACK FRAME, LIKE OTHER HARLEYS.

VRSC V-ROD

VRSCA V-Rod (2002–2006)
VRSCB V-Rod (2004–2005)
VRSCR Street Rod (2005–2007)
VRSCD Night Rod (2006–2008)
VRSCAW (2007–2010)
VRSCDX Night Rod Special (since 2007)
VRSCX (2007)
VRSCF V-Rod Muscle (since 2009)

2002 will be remembered as one of Harley-Davidson's most surprising years. Indeed, the VRSCA V-Rod was aimed primarily at new customers and, more to meet new pollution and noise standards than to continue providing a powerful engine, it adopted a new architecture. This V-Rod can be summed up simply: it was a Harley-Davidson with a custom look and a dragster character. Its "Revolution" engine, meanwhile, differed radically from the Milwaukee firm's past achievements.

This new 60 degree V-Twin engine was the first liquid-cooled motor on a mass-produced Harley-Davidson motorcycle. It featured double overhead camshafts on four-valve cylinder heads and a permanent magnet alternator. A veritable revolution, it was the result of a collaboration between Porsche and Harley-Davidson, but it also derived from the racing program and the Harley-Davidson VR-1000 Superbike. This 69 cubic inch (1130 cc) engine delivered 115 hp at 8250 rpm and a torque of 100 Nm at 7000 rpm. Double overhead camshafts, driven by hydraulic chain tensioners, controlled the high-speed four-valve heads, while an electronic fuel injection sequential port controlled the gas. Another innovation, a wet sump oil pump, implied that there was no external tank, while the clutch was hydraulically operated.

The large, stylized 2-1-2 exhaust offered a greater capacity for optimal performance while meeting noise requirements and still expressing

238-239 *The VRSCR Street Rod is an evolution of the VRSCA V-Rod, offering increased power, improved braking and a straight exhaust system.*

240-241 *The VRSCDX Night Rod Special reclaimed the configuration of the Night Rod but was now totally black, with a rear rim allowing the inclusion of a wide tire.*

the characteristic Harley-Davidson sound. Quintessentially modern, the Revolution engine was rubber-mounted on V-Rod silent blocks and equipped with a counterbalancing system that reduced internal vibration to the silver frame, which was also the first perimeter frame for Harley-Davidson. This concept provided better chassis rigidity and, as the aesthetic remained a key element for the brand, the hydroforming process created a frame seemingly free of soldering. The fuel tank was placed under the seat, which helps keep the weight close to the ground and maximizes fuel consumption. Thus, the two downdraft induction ducts and the high-speed air filter were just above the center of the engine, in the fuel tank's usual position, for a direct air intake. At the front, the headlight shape was topped by the support of the new shell-like dashboard, which featured a speedometer, tachometer, fuel gauge and fire hazard control. The instrumentation also included a self-diagnostic system. With a very low seat, at only 26 inches (660 mm), the V-Rod welcomed drivers of all sizes.

The VRSCA V-Rod diversified in 2004 with the VRSCB V-Rod. The VRSCB was simply a base V-Rod with a black frame and a different finish offered at a more attractive price. A VRSCR Street Rod became available early in 2005 in the U.S. and Europe. This straight V-Rod exhaust offered 5 extra horsepower compared to the VRSCA and VRSCB and had a 3-disc brake system and Brembo calipers.

In 2006, the V-Rod family was still composed of three models, but the VRSCB's substitute, the VRSCD Night Rod, used the Street Rod's straight exhaust, with a few improvements, to deliver 120 horsepower. All the V-Rods got a new frame and a tank that gained 1.3 gallons (5 liters) under the seat, increasing its capacity to 5 gallons (19 liters) of gasoline.

For 2007, the V-Rod family consisted of five models and it received significant changes. The base model, the VRSCA V-Rod, became the VRSCAW V-Rod, the W emphasizing its adoption of a 9-inch-wide (240 mm) rear tire. The new VRSCDX was a Night Rod Special that adopted an all-black decor and the wide rim of the VRSCAW, a transformation that neither the VRSCD Night Rod nor the VRSCR Street Rod benefited from. Even more radically, the new VRSCX brought the V-Rod engine displacement from 69 cubic inches (1130 cc) to 76 cubic inches (1250 cc) by simply increasing the bore. This VRSCX, known as a "Screamin' Eagle/Vance & Hines" V-Rod racing dragster, was produced in a limited edition of 1400 copies.

In 2008, the new 76 cubic inch (1250 cc) Revolution V-Twin engine was given to all the VRSCs, with an output of 123 hp and a torque of 11.5 daN.m. The VRSC series had an anti-dribbling clutch with a gentler operation. However, the VRSC family was composed of only three new models. Among the models that disappeared was the limited edition VRSCX, and while the VRSCR Street Rod was more present in the American and European lines, the Night Rod VRSCD base was only available in the American catalog.

The 2009 Power-Cruiser VRSC V-Rod line was again dramatically enriched with the VRSCF V-Rod Muscle. It had a large inverted fork, a large-capacity dual exhaust system, a sleek restyled rear end that enhanced its huge 9-inch (240 mm) tires and a square silhouette highlighted by meshed projecting vents that illustrated the power of the well-named V-Rod Muscle engine. The range that year consisted of the three same V-Rods in the U.S. and Europe, as the VRSCD Night Rod no longer existed.

The three VRSC V-Rod models were renewed for 2010 and remained virtually unchanged, but the base model, the VRSCAW V-Rod, was no longer available in 2011. The 2011 range consisted of the VRSCDX Night Rod Special and the VRSCF V-Rod Muscle, both for the U.S. and Europe.

243 THE V-ROD BLOCK ENGINE WAS STILL A V-TWIN HARLEY-DAVIDSON, BUT ITS ARCHITECTURE WAS NEW, WITH LIQUID-COOLED OPENED CYLINDERS AND DOUBLE OVERHEAD CAM SHAFTS.

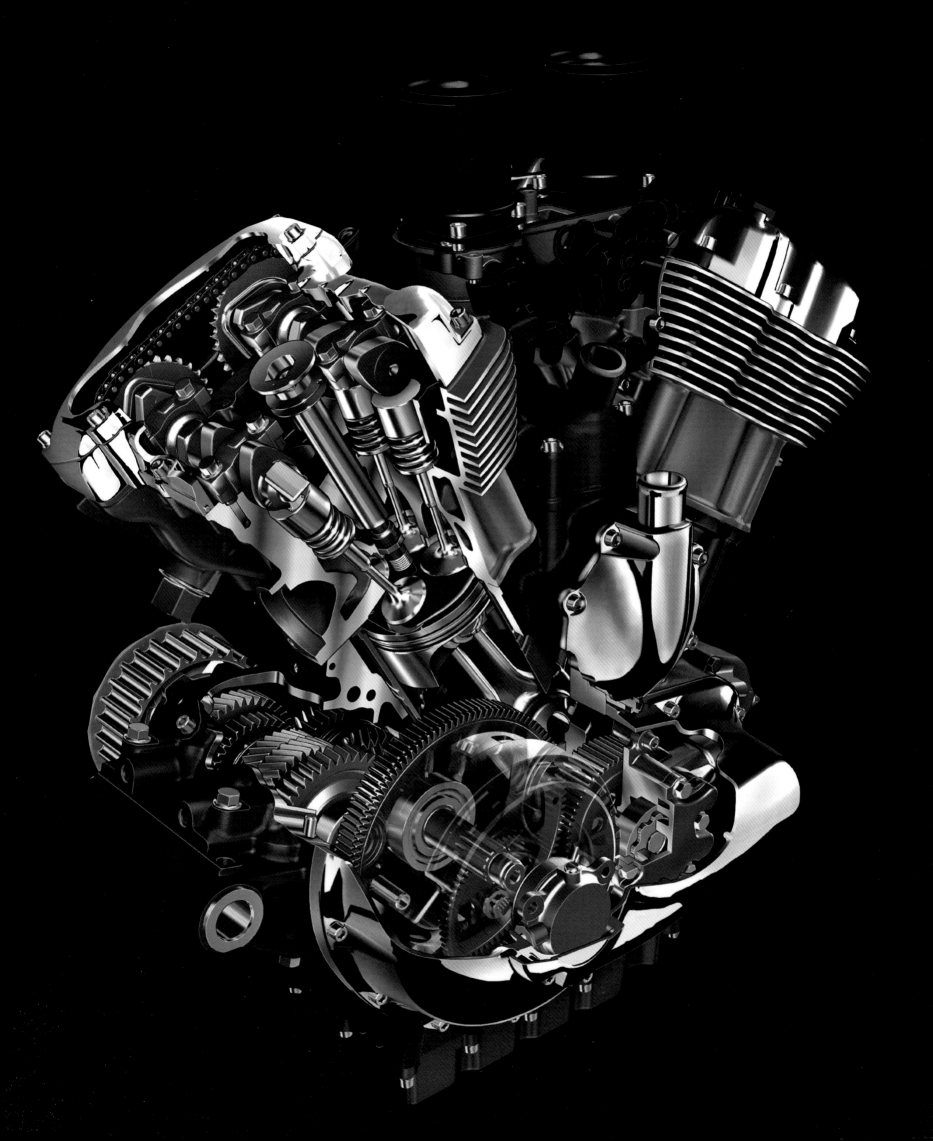

HARLEY-DAVIDSON CVO "CUSTOM VEHICLE OPERATION" SCREAMIN' EAGLE PROGRAM

1999: FRX2 Dyna Super Glide, FXR3 Dyna Super Glide

2000: FXR4 Dyna Super Glide, FLTRSEI Screamin' Eagle Road Glide

2001: FXDWG2 Dyna Wide Glide, FLTRSEI2 Screamin' Eagle Road Glide

2002: FXDWG3 Dyna Wide Glide, FLHRSEI Screamin' Eagle Road King

2003: FXSTDSE Screamin' Eagle Deuce, FLHRSEI2 Screamin' Eagle Road King

2004: FXSTDSE Screamin' Eagle Softail Deuce, FLHTCSE Screamin' Eagle Electra Glide

2005: FLSTFSE Screamin' Eagle Fat Boy, VRSCSE Screamin' Eagle V-Rod, FLHTCSE2 Screamin' Eagle Electra Glide 2

2006: FLSTFSE2 Screamin' Eagle Fat Boy, FLHTCUSE Screamin' Eagle Ultra Classic Electra Glide,

VRSCSE2 Screamin' Eagle V-Rod, VRXSE Screamin' Eagle V-Rod Destroyer

2007: FXDSE Screamin' Eagle Dyna, FXSTSSE Screamin' Eagle Softail Springer,

FLHRSE3 Screamin' Eagle Road King, FLHTCUSE2 Screamin' Eagle Ultra Classic Electra Glide

2008: FXDSE2 Screamin' Eagle Dyna, FXSTSSE2 Screamin' Eagle Softail Springer,

FLHRSE4 Screamin' Eagle Road King, FLHTCUSE3 Screamin' Eagle Ultra Classic Electra Glide

2009: FXDFSE CVO Dyna Fat Bob, FXSTSSE3 CVO Softail Springer,

FLHTCUSE4 CVO Ultra Classic Electra Glide, FLTRSE3 CVO Road Glide

2010: FXDFSE2 CVO Fat Bob, FLSTSE CVO Softail Convertible, FLHXSE CVO Sreet Glide,

FLHTCUSE5 CVO Ultra Classic Electra Glide, FLHTCUSE5-BLK CVO Ultra Classic Electra Glide Dark Side Limited Edition

2011: FLSTSE2 CVO Softail Convertible, FLHXSE2 CVO Street Glide,

FLHTCUSE6 CVO Ultra Classic Electra Glide, FLTRUSE CVO Road Glide Ultra

248 THE 2011 FLHXSE2 CVO STREET GLIDE IS EQUIPPED WITH SPEAKERS IN ITS LOWER FAIRING.

250 TOP THE 2003 FXSTDSE CVO DEUCE WAS A COMMEMORATIVE MODEL THAT CELEBRATED THE FIRST 105 YEARS OF HARLEY-DAVIDSON.

250-251 THE 2005 FLSTFSE CVO FAT BOY WAS THE FIRST SOFTAIL MODEL TO RECEIVE THE NEW 103 CUBIC INCH (1700 CC) "STROKER" ENGINE.

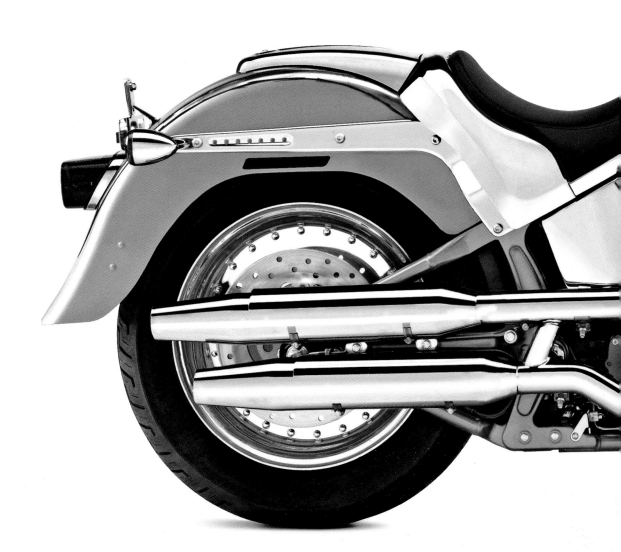

In 1999, Harley-Davidson launched the CVO program to meet the needs of a clientele wishing to buy customizable bikes from the Milwaukee firm. These bikes were produced in small quantities, with specialized, limited edition chrome, custom paint and unique accessories. Part of the allure was their exclusivity: it was impossible to get these special accessories from dealers to equip other Harley-Davidson models. Thus, if you needed to paint a motorcycle belonging to this program, you had to submit its CVO registration card.

Harley-Davidson designed and manufactured high performance Screamin' Eagle parts and accessories and made them available from dealers. It was with these parts that the first CVO bikes, dubbed the CVO Screamin' Eagle limited series, were designed in 1999. The first model was simply customized on a base Dyna Super Glide FXD. Nine hundred and fifty copies were made of this FXR2 in a solid color and another 950 were made of the two-tone FXR3. These two motorcycles had an 82 cubic inch (1340 cc) engine displacement.

The following year, in 2000, the company, still using the FXD Super Glide base, renewed the operation, offering a two-tone FXR4 Evolution with a 82 cubic inch (1340 cc) engine. One thousand copies were produced. But the CVO then offered a FLTRSEI based on a Road Glide with a 95 cubic inch (1550 cc) Twin-Cam 95 engine, and 1550 copies were brought to market. Changes to this FLTRSEI Road Glide, which had a chrome and silver engine, were made using specially designed Screamin' Eagle parts in order to be street legal. This kit notably included an increased bore, flathead pistons, special cams, a calibration different than the admission and another air filter. These changes increased the power by 10 percent and the torque by 14 percent. This Screamin' Eagle Road King also included more than $7500 (5475 euros) worth of parts and accessories and a unique paint. Starting that year, the CVOs were also imported into Europe.

The CVO program diversified in 2001, as success beckoned despite the high price of these custom bikes, and the FXR4 gave way to a FXD-WG2 made from a Dyna Wide Glide with an 88 cubic inch (1450 cc) Twin-Cam 88 engine. One thousand seven hundred copies of this motorcy-

cle were produced. Operation Road Glide was renewed with the FLTRSEI2, and 1750 units were produced.

In 2002 the Dyna Wide Glide FXDWG3, of which 1950 copies were manufactured, had the same engine displacement, while a Screamin' Eagle Road King replaced the Road Glide with a 95 cubic inch (1550 cc) Twin-Cam engine. Two thousand two hundred would be produced under the FLHRSEI name.

For the 100th anniversary year, the CVO produced 2950 copies of a FXSTDSE Screamin' Eagle Deuce built on the base of a Softail and powered by a 95 cubic inch (1550 cc) Twin-Cam 95 engine. They also produced 3200 copies of the FLHRSEI2 Screamin' Eagle Road King, but with a 103 cubic inch (1690 cc) Twin-Cam 103 engine.

CVO bikes performed very well and the operation revealed that customers primarily wanted high performance machines. For 2004, the

FXSTDSE Screamin' Eagle Softail Deuce was renewed with its 95 cubic inch (1550 cc) Twin-Cam 95 engine, while the Road King disappeared in favor of a new FLHTCSE Screamin' Eagle Electra Glide with a 103 cubic inch (1690 cc) engine that featured air and oil cooling.

In 2005, Harley-Davidson produced three CVO models to meet growing demand, and 2400 copies were made of the VRSCSE Screamin' Eagle, which had an increased 76 cubic inch (1250

252-253 THE 2005 FLHTCSE CVO ELECTRA GLIDE WAS PRODUCED, AS THE YEAR BEFORE, FROM AN ELECTRA GLIDE WITH A 103 CUBIC INCH (1700 CC) CAPACITY BENEFITING FROM AN OIL AND AIR COOLING SYSTEM.

254 top In 2005, the first CVO on a V-Rod base appeared with this VRSCSE high performance 76 cubic inch (1250 cc) engine, which is equipped with special parts.

254-255 Following the excitement generated by the CVO V-Rod, the 2006 VRSCSE CVO V-Rod incorporated the technical characteristics of the 2005 VRSCE with some minor cosmetic changes.

cc) engine capacity. Three thousand four hundred copies were made of the FLSTFSE Screamin' Eagle Fat Boy with a 103 cubic inch (1690 cc) Stroker engine, and 3700 FLHTCSE2 Screamin' Eagle Electra Glides were made, once again from an Electra Glide Classic with an increased 103 cubic inch (1690 cc) engine capacity.

CVOs were no longer anecdotal vehicles produced in small numbers, and although they remained in limited editions, from 2005 on they were integrated into the annual listing of Harley-Davidsons distributed in the company's dealerships.

The CVO family grew in 2006 with four new models. The 103 cubic inch (1690 cc) FLSTFE2 Screamin' Eagle Fat Boy and the 76 cubic inch (1250 cc) VRSCSE2 Screamin' Eagle V-Rod were renewed that year, while the 103 cubic inch (1690 cc) FLHTCUSE Screamin' Eagle Ultra Classic Electra Glide replaced the 2005 Electra Glide Classic. But the big news was the VRXSE Screamin' Eagle V-Rod Destroyer made from a 79 cubic inch (1300 cc) V-Rod engine and designed for drag racing competition.

The six-speed transmissions and new Harley-

Davidson engines appeared in 2007. The CVO models benefitted from these developments and saw their engine capacity increase. The VRSC V-Rod disappeared from the CVO operation and Harley-Davidson offered four models. Only three were imported into Europe, with the 110 cubic inch (1800 cc) FXDSE Screamin' Eagle Dyna still only available in the U.S. market.

The other models, which were all 110 cubic inches (1800 cc), included the FXSTSSE Screamin' Eagle Softail Springer, the FLHTCUSE2 Screamin' Eagle Ultra Classic Electra Glide and the FLHRSE3 Screamin' Eagle Road King. The base engines of these new bikes came from the 97 cubic inch (1584 cc) Twin-Cam 96, which saw its capacity increase to 110 cubic inches (1800 cc) by increasing the bore.

For 2008, the CVO Screamin' Eagle Harley-Davidson motorcycles were again produced in four models, including FL versions equipped with an original Harley-Davidson anti-lock braking system that was only an option on standard models. The FLHTCUSE3 Screamin' Eagle Ultra Classic Electra Glide, FHRSE4 Screamin' Eagle

Road King, FXDSE2 Screamin' Eagle Dyna and FXSTSSE2 Screamin' Eagle Softail Springer had the same base as the 2007 models and they kept the same 110 and 110B Twin-Cam engines.

The models varied somewhat in 2009, but they retained the same 110 cubic inch (1800 cc) engine. The FXSTSSE3 CVO Softail Springer and the FLHTCUSE4 CVO Ultra Classic Electra Glide kept the same base as the year before, but the FXDFSE CVO Dyna Fat Bob replaced the Dyna and the Road Glide made its comeback with the FLTRSE3 CVO Road Glide.

The 2010 edition kept the 110 cubic inch (1800 cc) engine but introduced a new concept for the CVO with the FLSTSE Softail Convertible, whose half-fairing, luggage and passenger seat were easily removable. The other new model, the FLHXSE CVO Street Glide, had larger saddle-bags than the base Street Glide and also LED flashers and an LED rear light.

The 2009 FXDFSE2 CVO Fat Bob and FLHT-CUSE5 CVO Ultra Classic Electric Glide were renewed for 2010. However, the FLHTCUSE5-BLK CVO Ultra Classic Electra Glide Dark Side Limited Edition model was limited to 999 copies and was added to the CVO line in January 2010. The bike was painted entirely black and featured a 110 cubic inch (1800 cc) engine, plus a six-speed transmission and a Garmin GPS.

The 2011 FLSTSE2 CVO Softail Convertible was equipped with a new sound system in a redesigned inner fairing. The music was supplied by an 8GB iPod nano housed in a protective pouch. Other new features included 1.25 inch (3 cm) welded "Mini-Ape" handlebars, cruise control, keyless ignition and anti-lock brakes. The 2011 FLHXSE2 CVO Street Glide, with a new 19-inch (48 cm) "Agitator" front wheel, featured new vented lower fairings that housed two of the six speakers included in the audio system, which incorporated an 8 GB iPod nano and its docking station.

The FLHTCUSE6 CVO Ultra Classic Electra Glide was equipped for 2011 with a hammock-style suspended dual-control heated seat with leather inserts. The chrome 2-1-2 dual exhaust ended with black mufflers, and there were new mirrors coated with chrome.

The new 2011 FLTRUSE CVO Road Glide Ultra was equipped with a Road Tech zumo 660 GPS navigation system, a sophisticated harman/kardon system with BOOM! Bagger speakers, an 8GB iPod nano and its docking station and a double suspended seat with dual control heating.

256-257 In 2007, the CVO family welcomed for the first time a model with a Springer fork: the 110 cubic inch (1800 cc) CVO FXSTSSE Springer Softail with a six-speed transmission.

258-259 *top* The third edition of the *FLTRSE3* CVO Road Glide model for 2009, this bike had the same design as the first model that appeared in 2000 but now had a more streamlined 110 cubic inch (1800 cc) engine and a slightly more streamlined design.

258-259 *bottom* In 2010, a new CVO concept appeared with the *FLSTSE* Softail Convertible. Its nose fairing, saddlebags and sissy bar could be dismantled quickly without tools to transform this road bike into a custom model.

260 top BASED ON THE DYNA SUPER GLIDE, THE 2008 FXDSE
CVO DYNA COMBINED THE EXCEPTIONAL PERFORMANCE OF THE
110 CUBIC INCH (1800 CC) ENGINE WITH THE ROAD FEATURES OF
THE SUPER GLIDE TO MAKE THIS BIKE A SPORTY ROAD MODEL.

260-261 THE 2010 FXDFSE CVO FAT BOB DYNA IS A MODEL
THAT IS DECIDEDLY HIGH PERFORMANCE, ASSERTING ITS
AGGRESSIVENESS WITH ITS EXHAUST, BIG WHEELS AND AIR FILTER.

262 PRODUCED IN 999 NUMBERED COPIES, THE 2010 CVO
FLHTCUSE5-BLK ULTRA CLASSIC ELECTRA GLIDE DARK SIDE
LIMITED EDITION HOUSED A GPS NAVIGATION SYSTEM BEHIND ITS
LITTLE SMOKED WINDSHIELD, IN ADDITION TO VERY COMPLETE
RADIO EQUIPMENT.

262-263 THE 2011 FLTRUSE CVO ROAD GLIDE ULTRA
OFFERS THE MOST COMPREHENSIVE AND LUXURIOUS EQUIPMENT
AND ELECTRONICS TO DRIVERS AND PASSENGERS. IT'S A VERY SAFE
MOTORCYCLE WITH A MASSIVE FAIRING FIXED TO THE FRAME FOR
A TRUE HIGH-END GT.

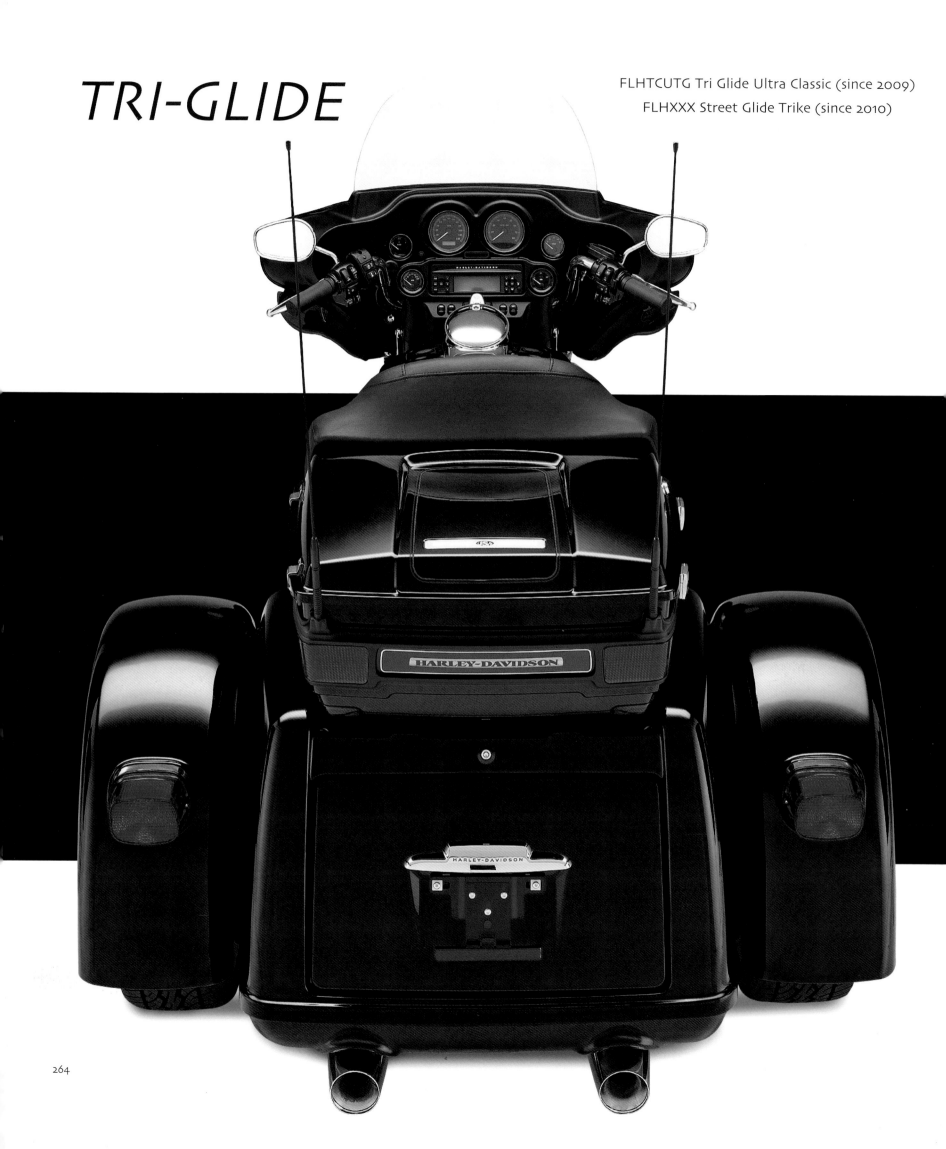

TRI-GLIDE

Among its new entries for 2009, Harley-Davidson offered the FLHT-CUTG Tri Glide Ultra Classic, a modern variation on the old Servi-Car that was produced until 1973. With the Tri Glide Ultra Classic, developed on the base of the new Touring Ultra Classic Electra Glide chassis, Harley-Davidson offered a tricycle that met the expectations of customers searching for a vehicle that was more stable than a motorcycle. The Tri Glide offered the same equipment as an Ultra Classic Electra Glide, but its frame was modified at the front to maintain good handling despite an extended fork and a caster angle that had been increased from the Touring's 29.25 degrees to 32 degrees. At the rear, the drive shaft was equipped with a differential and two adjustable pneumatic shocks. Secondary transmission remained assigned to a toothed belt and the reverse option was electric. The 103 cubic inch (1,690 cc) Twin-Cam used the same six-speed gearbox as the Touring, and the whole Tri Glide line, with its fork and trunk, remained similar to the Ultra Classic Electra Glide. The Tri Glide, however, was not imported into Europe.

To boost sales of this Trike concept in 2010, Harley-Davidson added a new three-wheeled model – the FLHXXX Street Glide Trike. The FLHXXX was offered at a price lower than the FLHTCUG Tri Glide Ultra Classic. Both Trikes were built from the same platform, but the Street Glide Trike used the lowered design of the Street Glide motorcycle while the fairing had a simple little deflector in place of the windshield. It was not equipped with a trunk. This Trike model was also not imported into Europe. Both Trike models, however, were renewed for 2011.

264 AND 265 THE FLHTCUTG TRI GLIDE ULTRA CLASSIC TRIKE, WHICH APPEARED WITH THE 2009 SERIES, IS POWERED BY A 103 CUBIC INCH (1700 CC) TWIN-CAM AND HAS EQUIPMENT SIMILAR TO THAT OF THE ULTRA CLASSIC ELECTRA GLIDE.

266-267 BEFORE HARLEY-DAVIDSON PRODUCED ITS TRIKES IN
2009, MANY HARLEY-DAVIDSON MOTORYCLES WERE
TRANSFORMED INTO TRIKES BY COMPANIES SUCH AS LEHMAN
TRIKES, WHICH OFFERED CONVERSION KITS. THIS CUSTOM MODEL
IS DERIVED FROM A HARLEY-DAVIDSON SOFTAIL.

THE AUTHOR

Born March 29, 1957, at Montereau in the department Seine-et-Marne, France, **Pascal Szymezak**, a journalist who specializes in motorcycles, began by collaborating with various periodicals and magazines related to motorcycling and motorcycle travel. He later became editor-in-chief for a monthly magazine that focused on the Harley-Davidson motorcycle, the new American models, the bikes' history and trips through the country. Since 1987 he has edited the *Nice-Matin*'s weekly column on motorcycles, and he collaborates on Hachette's Harley-Davidson motorcycle collection, including the *Joe Bar Team*. He is the author and co-author of various books on Harley-Davidson motorcycles, which he has regularly used since 1989 for his journeys through the American West and Far West. Since 1984 he has frequently visited the United States, not only for large-scale Harley-Davidson events such as Bike Week at Daytona Beach and the Sturgis and Laughlin rallies, but also to produce documentaries on Harley-Davidson models in Milwaukee, New York and Kansas City and on customization specialists throughout the U.S., from California to Florida, and even in Europe. He currently travels on a customized Harley-Davidson Softail Fat Boy 88 cubic inch (1450 cc). He is the author of *Harley Davidson: A Way of Life*, first published by White Star and in 1997 and followed by an updated revision and which has sold a total of 250,000 copies.

BIBLIOGRAPHY

The Big Book of Harley-Davidson
  Thomas C. Bolfert
  Harley-Davidson, Inc., 1989

Harley-Davidson The Milwaukee Marvel
  Harry V. Sucher
  Haynes Publishing Group Ltd, 1990

Inside Harley-Davidson An Engineering History of the Motor Company from F-Heads to Knuckleheads 1903-1945
  Jerry Hatfield
  Motorbooks International, 1990

Harley-Davidson Motorcycles 1903-1969: The Legend Begins
  Harley-Davidson
  Harley-Davidson, Inc., 1993

The Harley-Davidson Motor Company An Official Ninety-Year History
  David K. Wright
  Motorbooks International, 1993

Harley-Davidson Panheads
  Greg Field
  Motorbooks International, 1995

Harley-Davidson Data Book
  Rick Conner
  Motorbooks International, 1996

The Illustrated Directory of Harley-Davidson Motorcycles
  Tod Rafferty
  Salamander Books Ltd, 2001

100 Years of Harley-Davidson Advertising
  Thomas C. Bolfert
  Bulfinch Press, 2002

Standard Catalog of Harley-Davidson Motorcycles 1903-2003
  Doug Mitchel
  Krause Publications, 2004

Standard Catalog of American Motorcycles 1898-1981
  Jerry Hatfield
  Krause Publications, 2006

The Mechanical and Human History of the Harley-Davidson Sportster
  Pascal Szymezak
  E.T.A.I., 2009

INDEX

PHOTO CREDITS

20th Century Fox/Gerlitz, Ava V./Album/Contrasto: page 239
Alvey & Towers: pages 252-253
Bettmann/Corbis: page 18
www.bikephoto.co.uk: pages 6, 10-11, 16, 46 top, 46 bottom, 47, 48-49, 92, 92-93, 101, 181
Paul Buckley: pages 76-77, 78-79, 80-81, 112-113, 126-127, 174-175, 196-197
G. Cigolin/Archivio DeAgostini: pages 234, 237
John Dean/ Reynolds-Alberta Museum: pages 86-87, 96-97, 98-99, 150-151
Illustrated London News Ltd/Mary Evans: pages 22, 23
© photo paolograna@mclink.it: pages 120-121

Ron Kimball/KimballStock: pages 212-213, 266, 267
Dave King © Dorling Kindersley: pages 30-31, 58-59, 83, 116-117, 125, 128-129, 130-131, 136-137, 138-139, 140-141, 154-155, 172-173, 178-179, 210-211
Oleksiy Maksymenko/ Photolibrary.com: pages 4-5, 240-241
Pascal Szymezak: pages 2-3, 8, 12-13, 14-15, 19, 20, 20-21, 27 bottom, 32, 33, 88, 88-89, 94-95, 102, 132, 132-133, 134-135, 141, 145, 152-153, 154, 156, 158-159, 160-161, 162 top, 162 bottom, 164-165, 166-167, 168, 168-169, 170-171, 182-183, 184-185, 186-187, 188, 188-189, 190-191, 192-193, 194-195, 198, 200-201,

202-203, 204-205, 206-207, 208-209, 214, 216-217, 218-219, 219, 220-221, 222-223, 226-227, 228-229, 230-231, 232-233, 236-237, 238-239, 243, 244-245, 246-247, 248, 250, 250-251, 252-253, 254, 254-255, 256-257, 257, 258-259 top, 258-259 bottom, 260, 260-261, 262, 262-263, 264, 265
Tips Images: page 45
Courtesy of: Yesterdays Antique Motorcycles - www.yesterdays.nl: pages 1, 24, 24-25, 25 top left, 25 top right, 26, 27 top, 28-29, 34, 35, 36 top left, 36 top right, 36-37, 37, 38, 38-39, 39, 40, 41, 42-43, 43 top left, 43 top right, 43 bottom, 44,

50, 50-51, 51 top left, 51 top right, 52-53, 53 top, 53 center, 53 bottom, 54 top, 54 bottom, 54-55, 55 top, 56 top, 56-57 bottom, 57, 60, 60-61, 62, 63, 64-65, 65 top left, 65 top right, 66, 67, 68, 68-69, 69 top left, 69 top center, 69 top right, 70 top, 70 bottom, 71, 72, 72-73, 74, 74-75, 82, 84, 85 top, 85 bottom, 90, 90-91, 91 top, 103, 104 top left, 104 top right, 104 bottom, 105, 106, 106-107, 107, 108, 109, 110-111, 111 top, 111 bottom, 114, 115, 119, 122, 123 top, 123 bottom, 143 top, 143 center, 143 bottom, 146, 147, 148, 148-149, 149, 176, 177, 224 top, 224 bottom, 225

ACKNOWLEDGEMENTS

The copyright holder would like to thank Geert Versleyen of Yesterdays Antique Motorcycles, Netherlands, and the staff of Reynolds-Alberta Museum, Canada for their helpful collaboration.

Cover
A detail of the cylinders and fake tank of a 2005 VRSC V-Rod. © www.bikephoto.co.uk

Back cover
A 2008 FLSTC Heritage Softail Classic. © Pascal Szymezak

This edition published in 2014 by
CHARTWELL BOOKS
an imprint of Book Sales
a division of Quayside Publishing Group, Inc.
276 Fifth Avenue Suite 206
New York, New York 10001
USA

Translation: Salvatore Ciolfi
Editing: John Schaefer

ISBN 978-0-7858-3128-0

Printed in China